COLLEGE STYLE SHEET

Sixth Edition

JON FURBERG B.A., M.A.

RICHARD HOPKINS B.A., M.A.

49TH AVENUE PRESS

LANGARA COLLEGE, VANCOUVER, BRITISH COLUMBIA, CANADA

Jon Furberg
1944-1992

COLLEGE STYLE SHEET
Sixth Edition
Copyright © 2005 by Richard Hopkins and the Estate of Jon Furberg.
All rights reserved.

Publisher:
49th AVENUE PRESS
Langara College, 100 West 49th Avenue
Vancouver, BC V5Y 2Z6

Distributor:
BENDALL BOOKS
P.O. Box 115, Mill Bay, BC V0R 2P0
ELECTRONIC MAIL: admin@bendallbooks.com
WORLD WIDE WEB: www.bendallbooks.com
Fax: 250-173-2910

Sample essay pages reproduced with permission of Leslie Peeler, Jeff Webster, and Tim Hopkins.

Printed in Canada

LIBRARY AND ARCHIVES CANADA CATALOGUING IN PUBLICATION DATA
Furberg, Jon, 1944-1992.
    College style sheet/Jon Furberg, Richard Hopkins.- 6th ed.
    Includes index.
    ISBN 1-896661-06-8
    1. Authorship--Style manuals.   2. Report writing--Handbooks,
manuals, etc.   I. Hopkins, Richard, 1936-   II. Title.
PE11408..F87 2005   808'.027   C2005-90436-X

Contents

Preface & Acknowledgments

The *College Style Sheet* is guided in general by the standards of documentation presented by Joseph Gibaldi in the sixth and latest edition of the *MLA Handbook for Writers of Research Papers*, although it also includes guidelines contained in other pertinent texts, notably the *Publication Manual of the American Psychological Association* and *The Chicago Manual of Style* (see "Standards of Style," pages 10-11).

This edition of the *College Style Sheet* incorporates the most recent changes and additions contained in these style manuals, wherever they are applicable in this much shorter work. The *Style Sheet* recognizes that research essay conventions may not always suit all types of essays or the preferences of all instructors. Alternatives are therefore offered in some cases, usually accompanied by the recommendation that students consult their instructors about which style to follow. In this way, the *Style Sheet* admits, within limits, style variations that may be preferred in some academic departments.

∼

Langara Style Sheet was the heading on a folded, single-sheet documentation guide composed in 1974 by Alan Dawe, of the English department at the then Langara campus of Vancouver Community College. From this bare-bones beginning, it developed into a pamphlet, inspired by suggestions from students and faculty as they used the sheet in a variety of courses and disciplines. By 1983, it was widely used in colleges in British Columbia, and the name *College Style Sheet* was adopted. In the mid 1980s, departments other than English were offering descriptions of the documentation styles of their respective disciplines; and major changes were announced by the most influential arbiter of style, the Modern Language Association of America (MLA)—all these were addressed in the *Style Sheet's* 1988 edition. Throughout this process, we tried to maintain the spirit of brevity and simplicity of the original style sheet.

Over the years, a number of former colleagues from the Langara College English department have provided expert advice for the *Style Sheet:* Eric Ball, Cynthia Flood, Roger Holdstock, Ken MacMillan, Megan Otton, and Gordon

Pybus. College librarians Judy Growe, Liza Hutchison, and Alison Curtis provided invaluable help and kindly permitted me to refer to their student guide *Evaluating and Citing Internet Resources.* Jeff Webster, from Psychology, and Gerda Kraus, from Biology, provided advice pertinent to their disciplines.

My hearty thanks to all for their invaluable contributions. And special thanks, too, to publisher Raymond Bendall for his unfailing assistance, patience, and encouragement.

As ever, I owe a debt to the late John Furberg, admired colleague and friend. The *College Style Sheet* represents but a small part of his legacy as a teacher and writer.

Richard Hopkins
March 2005

Introduction

The *College Style Sheet* is not a composition text or a handbook of grammar, punctuation, and usage; it is a guide to help you present essays—especially research essays—according to current conventions of physical layout and documentation of sources. All assignments requiring a paper in which you make use of someone else's words, ideas, or data also require that you acknowledge your sources of these borrowings and your specific use of them.

Each discipline, or field of study, follows a particular system, or "style," for presenting research material and for directing the reader to the original location of this information. Careful study and imitation of the appropriate conventions outlined here will save you hours of trial and error, and should result in improved grades.

~

Some frequently used terms need clarification. The word *style* signifies the way source material is presented and documented; it does not refer to the quality of your expression. By style is meant the accepted conventions regarding the form and placement of quotations, references to sources (whether quoted, paraphrased, or summarized), bibliographic citations, page layout and numbering, title pages, and the like.

The word *text* means the body of your essay—your words plus quotations and parenthetical references. A *reference* is the specific acknowledgment of your use of an external source of information or opinion; it may appear directly in your sentence, indirectly in a parenthesis, or in a note. The purpose of a reference is to direct the reader to a corresponding citation.

A *citation* is the full, formal statement of the publishing details for each source. Citations appear in alphabetical order in a bibliographic list (variously called "Works Cited," "References," "Bibliography," or "Literature Cited") that is placed at the end of the essay.

Remember that when your essay makes any use of secondary material, you are "doing research," and conventions govern the way you should acknowledge it. Ask each of your instructors which sections of the *Style Sheet* are pertinent to his or her assignments. Do not attempt to invent your own style. Treat your essay as though you were offering it for publication.

ESSAY
ESSENTIALS

Standards of Style

Academic disciplines rely upon certain standard manuals for models that demonstrate the accepted forms of quotations, references, and source citations.

English

Under the influence of the Modern Language Association of America (MLA) English faculties have abandoned footnotes and bibliography in favour of parenthetical references and a list of works cited, for the acknowledgment of sources in essay writing. The *College Style Sheet* summarizes the main features of this style. For a full discussion, consult:

> Gibaldi, Joseph. *MLA Handbook for Writers of Research Papers.* 6th ed. New York: Mod. Lang. Assoc., 2003.

This work should be available for quick consultation at the reference desk of your campus library, on short-term loan at the reserve desk, or for sale in the campus bookstore.

Psychology

Psychology papers employ a system of parenthetical references that stress author and date. The style authority is:

> American Psychological Association. *Publication Manual of the American Psychological Association.* 5th ed. Washington, DC: Amer. Psychological Assn., 2001.

The rudiments of APA style are presented in this *Style Sheet* (beginning on page 91) together with a sample text page and list of references. For further information, consult the full *Manual.* For brief, straightforward guidelines to the citing of Internet sources in APA style, consult the following:

> *APA Style.org: Electronic References. 2003.* APA PsychNET. 3 June 2005 <http://www.apastyle.org/elecref.html>.

Note: the angle brackets, <>, in the above citation are an MLA convention and are not part of the Internet address.

Sociology and Biology

Both disciplines use variations of basic APA style that are illustrated here (see pages 95 and 96) with examples and notes on distinguishing features. For more information on citing sources in Sociology, consult the following, available in your campus library:

> *American Sociological Association Style Guide.* 2nd ed. Washington, DC: Amer. Sociological Assn., 1997.

History and Political Science

These disciplines have tended to retain the traditional footnote style, with some modern variations. The MLA offers its own version of conventions for note style, but for many academics the most authoritative source is:

> *The Chicago Manual of Style.* 15th ed. Chicago: U of Chicago P, 2003.

This text should be available at the library reference desk and in the campus bookstore. The note style is discussed on pages 101-108 of this *Style Sheet.*

~

For further information and advice on documentation and style issues, access your campus library Web site and follow the appropriate links.

Evaluating and Citing Internet Research

The vast amount of information available on the Internet presents both an opportunity and a challenge to students doing research. With a few clicks of a mouse, you will be able to access a previously unimaginable number of potential research sources; but you will also need to evaluate these sources with particular care.

As with other kinds of research, the best place for you to begin is your campus library. Academic libraries pay substantial annual fees so that students can access online resources (books, articles, encyclopedias, etc.) for which payment is required. These resources are technically "on the Web," but you can only get at them if someone has paid on your behalf. By making these subscription materials available, your campus library is offering at least some guarantee of their reliability.

"Free" Web sources carry no such endorsement. Individuals, social agencies of all kinds, governments, educational institutions, businesses and corporations all put free information on the Web because they want as many people as possible to know about their ideas, services, or products. They may or may not have an ulterior motive. You should be especially wary, therefore, of material found on the "free Web." To try to determine its reliability, you can do the following:

1. Investigate the credentials of the author of a Web document. Use a search engine to find background information on the author; look up the author's name in library catalogues and article databases; or consult your instructor about the author's reputation.
2. Use e-mail or the telephone to find out more about an organization associated with a Web document.
3. Check to determine whether the purpose of the Web material you have found is to promote a product or cause. Promotional material may have a distinct bias.

4. See if the facts presented in a Web document are trustworthy by checking them against the facts presented in a known-reputable print or online source.[1]

Remember, too, that wide though its scope may be, the Internet has its limitations. Most of the content in libraries has *not* been posted free on the Web. The costs involved for labour, computer equipment, and copyright permissions are just too great. So combine your Internet research with print and media research and employ a range of sources to lend authority to your essay writing.

As you do your Internet research, you should record relevant publishing details for your works-cited list (see page 63). This can sometimes be troublesome as Internet sources may lack particular items (e.g., page numbers), and are subject to change in ways that print sources are not. As the *MLA Handbook* says, "writers must often settle for citing whatever information is available to them" (Gibaldi 208). One safeguard is to download or print the material you have found. Then, if the source disappears, at least you have proof of its previous existence, as well as a record of its publishing details.

Some Web sites offer a choice of formats for downloading and printing. The PDF (portable document format) version of, for example, a journal article will reproduce the typography, page numbering, and design of the original document, much like a photocopy. Because of (current) limitations of the format, the HTML (hypertext markup language) version will reproduce some features of the original but not others; graphics and illustrations may be stripped from the text. To look at PDF files you will need Adobe Acrobat software. Acrobat Reader is downloadable free at the Adobe Web site: <http://www.adobe.com/>.

For further advice about Internet research, access your campus library Web site and follow the appropriate links.

---

1. Judy Growe, Liza Hutchison, and Alison Curtis, *Evaluating and Citing Internet Resources* (Vancouver: Langara Coll. Lib., 2005) 5.

Word Processing

The use of computers and word-processing software is of enormous help in the preparation of essays. A full-featured word processor can offer a wide range of options. These tools will not magically transform you into a better writer, but they can certainly help with the rewriting and formatting of your work.

Here are some guidelines for users of word processors:

1. Take the time to learn your software, especially its editing and formatting features. Simple cut, copy, and paste routines can speed the rewriting and rearranging of text. Page formats (including details such as margin setting) and paragraph styles (specifying indentation, spacing, and alignment) can be defined (although default settings are usually suitable). Once established, these definitions can be saved and used on future papers. In the long run, you will not regret spending some time with your software manual and reading the "help" information provided with the program.

2. Use a 12-point standard typeface or font, such as Courier, which is used in the sample essay pages in this book, or Times New Roman. Stay away from fancy script or other "designer" fonts which are inappropriate for text.

3. Leave your right margins "ragged," as both MLA and APA style guidelines require, and do not use your word processor's auto-hyphenation tool.

4. Your word-processing software will be able to create italic type which, in published material, is used to distinguish book and other separately published titles, foreign words, and added emphasis. The APA and Chicago manuals endorse this use of italics, but the *MLA Handbook* prefers underlining as being more "distinctive" (Gibaldi 94) for use in essay writing. Your choice will depend upon the courses you are taking. In English, History, and Political Science courses, use underlining; in Psychology and Science courses, use italics. If in doubt, consult your instructor.

5. All full-featured word-processing programs include a spell-checker. Always use it, but never rely on it completely. If only one typographical error is found and corrected, it is worth the time taken, and you will be a little closer to the always elusive goal of a "letter-perfect" paper. But the

spell-checking software cannot be a substitute for your own careful proof-reading. The computer will not notice that you typed "form" instead of "from," or "too" instead of "two." It is advisable to proofread from a printed copy of the text rather than a screen copy; text on paper is easier to work with.

If your software permits, learn how to build a custom dictionary. This can be especially helpful if you are writing a number of papers on similar topics. Your custom dictionary can hold a variety of specific terms and proper nouns which appear frequently in your writing but are not in the program's main dictionary. The software will then ignore those "custom" words, and the spell-checking process will go faster.

6. Always, always, *always* make backup copies of your work. While writing, frequently save your work to your hard disk. Whenever you finish a session on the computer, also save a copy of your work to a backup disk. Then, should the computer or the hard-disk drive malfunction, your work can be retrieved using another machine. If you are working on a lengthy paper that may go through a series of drafts, you may want to "save as" and keep separate backup copies of each major revision. That way, material used in your first draft, but discarded in the second draft, can always be reinstated in your third draft.

Types of Essays

Before beginning a writing assignment, determine what type of essay you are expected to produce. Make sure you know the desired length and scope of the essay, and stick to the limits imposed by your instructor. Does the essay require quotations and references? Should it merely report existing information and ideas? Or are you to offer a *thesis* of your own—the key idea you present to the reader and support by using examples, logically developed arguments, and often research material as well?

Except where noted below, avoid the first-person pronoun, "I," in your essays. Any sentence can be rewritten to remove the self-conscious "I," "me," "my," "mine." It is not necessary to write, "In my opinion," "I believe," "I feel," etc., since the reader assumes your authorship. Similarly, it is redundant, and dull, to begin an essay with a statement of intention such as, "In the following essay, I shall try to prove...."

Personal Experience Essay

In some courses, you may be asked to narrate an event in your life that illustrates a significant truth you have discovered. In this case, write from a first-person point of view (using "I," "me," etc.), and employ vivid sensory language to help draw your reader into the scene. Dialogue is often a valuable means of dramatizing your story; if you use dialogue, imitate the conventions of paragraphing, punctuation, and quotation employed in published short stories or novels.

Expository Essay

A common assignment in many introductory English courses is a short expository essay (about five paragraphs, 350-600 words) in which you either offer information or explain your point of view on a topic you already know about.

These two general kinds of exposition vary according to your intention. One mainly gives information ("Why People Pray"); the other mainly defends an opinion ("Why Prayer Should [or Should Not] Be Permitted in Public Schools"). Here, the intent of each essay is obvious from its title.

Typically, a short expository essay begins with a paragraph that announces the *topic* (subject matter) and builds to a *thesis statement* in which you state your point of view. Then follows the middle portion of your text, consisting of three or more paragraphs of supporting evidence and reasoned discussion based mainly on your personal knowledge, experience, and judgment (but not necessarily excluding material from secondary sources). The essay ends with a paragraph that restates the thesis more emphatically and possibly suggests wider implications. A good ending does not merely summarize.

Research Essay

Unlike an expository essay, a research essay *must* present information and ideas gathered from a variety of sources outside your own knowledge and experience. You must consult and use other people's work. In some sense, all learning is the product of research: our understanding of the world develops and changes as we talk with others, read newspapers, magazines, and books, watch films and television, surf the Internet, and observe and react to events around us. When we want to know the answer to an important question, we often find we have to seek help in a source outside ourselves.

In a formal research essay, you must offer a well-developed thesis supported by convincing evidence and opinion found in appropriate sources that are acknowledged in your text and given credit with full citations in a bibliographic list placed at the end of the essay.

Basically, there are two kinds of research. "Primary research" generates new or up-to-date information from interviews, experiments, surveys, or other direct observations. "Secondary research" relies upon already published information and ideas found mainly in books, scholarly journals and magazines, on the Internet, and on audiotapes, videotapes, CD-ROMs, microforms, and so on. Although many assignments require secondary research alone, some combine the two kinds.

Through research you enlarge your knowledge and understanding of a subject and thus your capacity to draw intelligent, forceful conclusions. Some assignments ask only that you prove you have understood a problem; others, that you commit yourself to a solution.

Research essays regularly employ quotation, paraphrase, and summary, accompanied by appropriate acknowledgment of their sources. Sometimes other aids such as graphs, tables, and diagrams are helpful. Your research, from a *variety* of reliable sources (one or two are insufficient), must be incorporated logically as the essay develops. The key is to keep your thesis in mind always. What are you trying to illustrate? What are you trying to prove?

Try to find sources that are authoritative whenever you do research (particularly when using the Internet)—some instructors will turn to your bibliographic list to see how current and full your research has been, even before they read your text.

Literary Insight Essay

English courses in short fiction, poetry, drama, film, and the novel require papers in which you interpret, and perhaps evaluate, a work of literary or cinematic art. There are several ways you can read and usefully discuss a work of literature or any other art form: (1) as a created thing, interesting in itself; (2) as a mirror of significant truths about the external world; (3) as a stimulus that calls forth inner feelings and self-awareness; and (4) as the expression of an artist with unique skills, intelligence, and character.

Your instructor may ask only for a personal interpretation of the work at hand. In this case, you are doing primary research; the essay offers your own "insight" without reference to published criticism. You should paraphrase, summarize, and quote the literary text with sufficient frequency to illustrate the key points of your analysis. In-class essay tests are of this kind, as are some at-home papers. Remember that *your insight is your thesis.*

Term papers usually require that you do secondary research—finding agreement, controversy, and a variety of different approaches to the same work, or author, to provide support for your own point of view. By consulting, citing, and quoting pertinent critical works, you give your essay greater authority.

Technical Essay

Science courses sometimes require essays in which you record observations, experiments, data, etc., to illustrate your understanding of a particular scientific principle. You may have to describe a procedure, explain a law, or define a certain term.

Research Report

Research reports and research essays share a common purpose—to present the reader with interesting and useful information drawn from primary and/or secondary sources. But whereas essays are intended mainly for a general audience, reports are aimed at a more specific, more knowledgeable audience. Moreover, report texts are usually organized in sections under subheadings keyed to a table of contents rather than being continuous, like most essays, and they are more likely to contain tables and graphic illustrations.

Report assignments can be of several different kinds. For example, following a field-trip, survey, or interview you may be asked to write an objective account of your findings. Depending on the course and the instructor, you may have to offer your own conclusions.

In business courses, you may have to prepare a report analyzing a business problem or marketing opportunity, putting forward recommendations and perhaps a plan for their implementation. The emphasis is on concise presentation of practical information tightly organized under subheadings. A one-page abstract or "executive summary" precedes the text and provides a brief overview of its content.

Book Report

In some courses, you will read a book and then summarize its content in a book report. Or you may be asked to read several publications—books, articles, reports, etc.—and then outline what the authors said, perhaps evaluating your findings as well.

Summary

In a summary you condense the content of an article or excerpt from a longer work into 20-30 percent (or some other prescribed percentage) of its original length. For instance, you may summarize a 500-word article in 100 to 150 words. *In your own words*, you restate only the thesis, main points, and conclusion. Occasionally you may use a term or phrase that cannot be altered without losing an essential meaning. Omit the author's specific examples and illustrations. A summary is a miniature of the original—briefer and simpler. It presents only the main ideas, from the author's point of view, showing that you clearly understand what you have read. *Write as though you are that author.* You should never say, "I think . . ." or "In my opinion . . ." or anything that indicates you are writing from your own point of view. A summary tests your ability to read with understanding, not to judge.

Critique

In some courses, such as Philosophy, you may be asked to criticize (analyze and evaluate) an author's argument or point of view. Begin by summarizing the passage in your own words, showing the various steps the author has taken in building toward a conclusion. If you agree with the overall statement, try to extend it, using your own examples; if you disagree, give good reasons. Some instructors permit the use of the first-person "I" in critique writing.

~

Conventions of style vary for different kinds of essays in different disciplines. Though largely devoted to MLA style, this manual describes and exemplifies several other commonly used styles. When you are given an essay assignment, ask your instructor about which style you should use.

Parts of Essays

Title Page

The *MLA Handbook* says that a separate title page is not needed for research essays. It stipulates that title pages be combined with first text pages, as follows:

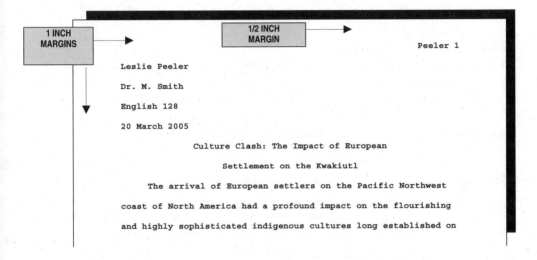

In this example, the student's last name appears half an inch from the top of the page, followed by the page number, and flush with the right margin. This combination of name and page number forms a running headline which appears in the same position on all subsequent pages. Next, the names of the student, instructor, and course, followed by the date, are double spaced beginning one inch from the top of the page and flush with the left margin. The essay title is centred, beginning a double space below the date, and is not in all capital letters (the rules for capitalizing are in item 10 on page 64). The first paragraph, indented half an inch or five spaces, begins a double space below the title with one-inch margins to left and right.

It is quite possible, however, that your instructors will ask you to provide a separate title page for your research essays as well as for other kinds of essays, too (if in doubt, ask). To prepare a separate title page, take a single, unlined sheet of paper and on it place the title of the essay in ALL CAPITAL letters, your name and student registration number, the course and section, your instructor's name, the name of your college or university, and the date. Imitate the order, arrangement, and spacing of the sample layout on page 29. Leave the back of the title page blank.

Title

The title presents the first words a reader encounters, so it is very important. Make it accurate and specific—and, if possible, catchy.

RESEARCH ESSAY

is not a title at all; it merely indicates a general kind of essay.

THE HUDSON'S BAY COMPANY

could be the title of a hefty volume; it has far too much scope for a term paper.

THE HUDSON'S BAY COMPANY AS A COLONIAL POWER, 1670-1770

is better, because it makes a specific promise about the essay's contents. An effective title invites the reader to resolve a conflict, explore a topic, discover a meaning.

For a term paper, a *subtitle* can help by providing additional information, as in the examples below. Note that both title layouts use a colon to precede the subtitle.

COLLATERAL DAMAGE: HOW MILITARY EUPHEMISMS
AFFECT OUR PERCEPTION OF WARFARE

Note: this subtitle provides further details to explain a vague title and clarify the true subject.

UNBORN DRUNKS:
THE TRAGEDY OF FETAL ALCOHOL SYNDROME

Note: here emotional language suggests an appeal to feelings and social awareness.

Perhaps you are writing about a published work and wish to include its title as part of your own. If it is separately published (e.g., a book, film, work of art, play, or television program), underline (or italicize; see item 4 on page 14) that part of your title:

ANIMAL SYMBOLISM IN FINDLEY'S <u>THE WARS</u> (book)

ALLUSIONS TO CHRISTIAN MYTH IN <u>FIELD OF DREAMS</u> (film)

THE TRIUMPH OF WOMEN IN ARTEMISIA GENTILLESCHI'S <u>JUDITH BEHEADING HOLOFERNES</u> (painting)

If you include the title of a poem, song, short story, essay, magazine or newspaper article, scholarly paper, or any other *part* of a longer work, place it in double quotation marks:

POETIC ELEMENTS IN COHEN'S LYRIC FOR "FAMOUS BLUE RAINCOAT" (song)

DECODING THE DECEPTION: ARENDT'S "LYING IN POLITICS" (essay)

Avoid a title that is a complete sentence. Instead, use a phrase—a hint rather than a flat statement. Do not place a period after your title (or after any other heading or subheading).

Contents

A table of contents is used only for reports or long essays that require several distinct parts identified by subheadings. It should appear on a separate, un-numbered page, following the title page. It lists the subheadings and their accompanying page numbers. Label the page Contents centred at the top, and word the list and the subheadings in the text identically.

Epigraph

You may wish to put a finishing touch on your essay by attaching an epigraph—a striking, pertinent quotation that helps prepare the reader's mind for the text that immediately follows. For essays with MLA-style title pages, insert the epigraph, centred and double spaced, between the title and the first line of text. For an essay with a separate title page, centre the epigraph three inches from the top of another separate sheet which you then insert between the title page and the first page of text. Do not use quotation marks. Place the name of the author below the epigraph flush right, followed by the title of the work. Do not include bibliographic details about the source of the quotation.

Text

The text of your essay should consist of connected paragraphs logically developed to create a coherent structure: beginning, middle, and end. It will contain some or all of the following: thesis statement, research information, arguments, ideas, opinions, quotations, paraphrases, and summaries. With the exception of the quotations, the entire text should be in your words.

Do *not* indicate a new paragraph by leaving an extra line space. Instead, indent the first line of each paragraph half an inch or five spaces. Double space the text throughout the essay (unless you are required to single space block quotations—see "Lengthy Quotations," page 41.)

An essay text is usually continuous. Still, as noted above, long essays or reports sometimes require subheadings. If so, put these in upper and lower case letters, underlined, and centred on the page with an extra line space above.

Illustrations and Tables

A graph, diagram, picture, or table should appear where it most logically fits—preferably right after the first mention of it in the text. Do not include illustrations unless your assignment clearly requires them; and do not include them without introducing them in the text.

If you use several graphs or diagrams, number them with arabic numerals: `Fig. 1`, `Fig. 2`, etc. Place this label *below* the illustration, starting at the left margin; continue on the same line with a simple caption; then add a full citation to indicate the source. Double space the caption if more than one line is needed.

For tables, place the heading `Table` on a line of its own *above* the material and against the left margin; add an arabic numeral if you use more than one table; leave a line space, and start the descriptive caption at the left margin, double spaced if it runs to more than one line; include a full citation immediately *below* the table after `Source:`, also at the left margin.

Appendix

An appendix appears at the end of the essay, immediately following the text, under the centred heading `Appendix`. It may include a graph, table, or other documentary material too extensive to put in the body of the essay without breaking its continuity. Indicate an appendix with a parenthetical note in your text at the place you want the reader to refer to it, e.g., (see Appendix). If you use more than one, add arabic numerals to the headings and to the text references, e.g., (see Appendix 2).

Content Notes (MLA Style)

Content notes provide source information, or comment, or explanation that cannot be accommodated within the text. Use them *sparingly*: the information they contain must be of fundamental interest.

To incorporate a single content note (assuming you are documenting with parenthetical text references, not footnotes) place a superscript (half a space above the line) arabic numeral [1] immediately after the item you wish to comment upon. If the note is brief, write it, double spaced, one letter space after a matching full-sized numeral two line spaces below the text on the same page (see page 103 for layout of footnotes). If the note is lengthy, or is accompanied by other content notes, place it under the heading `Notes` on a separate page immediately following the last text page. Number successive notes consecutively throughout the text using arabic superscripts.

Here is a sample note:

> 1. As Lewis Mumford says, in <u>Herman Melville</u>, "one might garner a whole book of verse from Moby-Dick" (181). W.O. Matthiessen, in <u>American Renaissance</u> (426), goes further and actually sets out lines in blank verse form.

If you are using the note style of documentation, combine your content notes with your reference notes and number them together. Place the notes at the foot of the appropriate pages or, alternatively, gather them as endnotes on a separate page following the text, according to your instructor's requirements. (See "The Note Style of Documentation," beginning on page 101.)

Works Cited (MLA Style)
This is a list of *all* the sources you made use of in your text, including media and Internet sources such as audiocassettes, television programs, films, online documents, etc. Whenever you use someone else's work in any way, except to confirm common knowledge, you *must* supply *both* a text reference *and* a corresponding works-cited entry. This rule applies to material you have paraphrased or summarized, as well as to material you have quoted.

Arrange all the entries in a single, alphabetized list on a separate sheet headed Works Cited and placed immediately following the last page of text. (See pages 94 and 105 for descriptions of how to present entries in APA and note styles.)

Presentation of Essays

Appearance *is* important. A well-presented essay gives the reader confidence that the writer has essential aspects of the writing process under control. The presence of even minor mechanical errors (see "Handling Mechanical Details" beginning on page 31), or spacing and layout problems, may cause the reader to doubt the writer's reliability. In preparing your essay, follow the guidelines set out below and imitate the sample on page 29:

1. Use 8½ x 11 inch good-quality, white paper.
2. Use one side of the paper only; leave the other side blank. Use a 12-point standard typeface (see item 2 under "Word Processing," page 14).
3. Double space the lines of text.
4. Left justify the text, leaving your right margin "ragged." Be sure that your text is sharp and black.
5. When page numbering an MLA-style research essay, use running headlines containing your last name and the page number set flush against the right margin. However, depending on the kind of essay you are writing, and the level of the course for which it is required, you may not need to follow research-essay style (if in doubt, consult your instructor). In which case, prepare a separate title page (see page 22 for guidelines); then count

Sample Alternative Title Page

2 INCHES →

CULTURE CLASH: THE IMPACT OF EUROPEAN

SETTLEMENT ON THE KWAKIUTL

1½ INCHES →

Leslie Peeler

98102385

English 128

Section 1

Dr. M. Smith

Northwest Community College

20 March 2005

1½ INCHES →

but *do not put the number on* the first text page (page 2 of the text is thus the first numbered page). Omit your name, and either centre the page number or place it against the right margin. For both types of essays, number the pages consecutively, including pages for endnotes, appendices, and works cited. Do not punctuate the numbers.

6. Some instructors like to receive essays that are stapled in the top left-hand corner; others prefer a folder (in which case put your name, the course, and the section number on the outside cover). If in doubt, ask.

7. If you present your essay in a folder, leave a 1½-inch margin at the left side of the page to allow for hole punching. Leave a 1-inch margin elsewhere. If you staple the pages at the top left-hand corner, leave a 1-inch margin all round.

8. Be sure to proofread your text carefully. For minor last-minute corrections, use the proofreader's symbols shown below (your instructor may use them when marking your essay).

9. Be sure to save a backup copy of your essay—it is rare, but not unknown, for an instructor to lose a student's essay.

Sample Text Page (MLA Style)

> ½ INCH

> 1 INCH MARGINS

and, of course, several kinds of salmon (Codere 57).

Christine Hunt-Peeler, herself a Kwakiutl, says that the Fort Rupert groups were and are regarded as the highest ranking as their village located at the northern end of Vancouver Island, adjacent to Queen Charlotte Strait, is where the Kwakiutl originated.

> DOUBLE SPACE TEXT

> INDENT ½ INCH or 5 SPACES

Social organization among the Kwakiutl was based mainly on rank, and rank was acquired by the giving of potlatches. A concise definition is given by Rohner:

> INDENT 1 INCH or 10 SPACES

> Potlatches may be described . . . as a congregation of people who are invited to publicly witness and later validate a host's claims to or transmission of hereditary privileges, and to receive in return, each according to his rank, differential amounts of wealth. (95)

> 1 SPACE AFTER BLOCK QUOTE

Potlatches were given for any "critical life event," for instance birth, adoption, puberty, marriage, and death (Rohner 95). They were also given as penalties for "breaches of ceremonial taboo such as laughing, stumbling or coughing at winter dances" (Barnett, qtd. in Rohner 95). Face-saving potlatches were held if misfortune occurred, say the capsizing

> 1½ INCHES IF PAGES IN FOLDER

> 1 INCH MARGINS

This sample page is a guide for the final draft of an MLA-style research essay employing parenthetical references. It shows the page number (i.e., page 10) as part of the running headline. (Ask your instructor if you need to follow this particular convention.) The text is *double* spaced as is the block quotation which is indented one inch (or ten spaces) from the left margin. Note the text references and the placement of the parentheses. The Hunt-Peeler reference in the second paragraph is to an interview, so no page number appears.

Here are some of the most commonly used proofreader's symbols :

Margin Symbol	Text Symbol

<table>
<tr><td></td><td>or
insert word_∧phrase</td></tr>
<tr><td>ℐ</td><td>delete ~~word or~~ phrase</td></tr>
<tr><td></td><td>change
~~correct~~ a word or phrase</td></tr>
<tr><td></td><td>move a∨word or phrase (misplaced)</td></tr>
<tr><td>stet</td><td>restore original text</td></tr>
<tr><td>l.c.</td><td>make /ower case</td></tr>
<tr><td></td><td>close up sp⌣ace</td></tr>
<tr><td>#</td><td>separate|words (add space)</td></tr>
<tr><td>trs</td><td>transpose letters words or</td></tr>
<tr><td>¶</td><td>begin new paragraph</td></tr>
<tr><td>no ¶</td><td>no new paragraph</td></tr>
</table>

Handling Mechanical Details

In polishing your final draft, pay close attention to the many mechanical details that need to be checked. For full discussion and exemplification of them, see the *MLA Handbook* or the APA *Manual*. Meanwhile, here are some items that regularly draw criticism when mishandled.

1. Spell out whole numbers that can be expressed in one or two words (e.g., eight, twenty-seven, two hundred), and use numerals for the rest (e.g., 8½, 127, 3,420). Spell out a number that begins a sentence. Retain numerals where they occur in names or titles (e.g., 49th Avenue). Use numerals also for dates, times, measurements, and money. Avoid mixing numerals and spelled-out numbers (use all numerals, e.g., 8½ by 11, not 8½ by eleven).
2. In science essays, decimal numbers less than 1 should be preceded by a zero (e.g. 0.563, not .563).
3. The simplest way to write a date is 4 July 1976, but July 4,1976 is acceptable (be consistent in your usage). Write 62 BC (or BCE, "before the common era"), but AD 85 (or 85 CE, "common era").
4. Underline (MLA style) or italicize (APA and Chicago style) the title of a book, magazine, newspaper, film, play, opera, long poem, radio or television program, record album (LP), compact disc (CD), laser disc, digital video disc (DVD), CD-ROM, computer diskette, audio- or videocassette, or audiotape. Underline or italicize foreign words that are not part of our ordinary speech. In MLA style, use quotation marks to indicate a part within a whole: a chapter, short story, short poem, article, essay, aria, or song title. In APA style, use quotation marks when a title appears in the text, but not when it is in the list of references.
5. Use abbreviations in your notes and works-cited entries, but avoid them in your text, except for conventional forms such as "a.m.," "Mr.," "RCMP," and "UN." In your text, spell out the names of months and measurements such as "inch," "pound," and "metre." Except in well-known cases (such as NATO), spell out the name of an organization on first use, and place the ab-

breviation in a parenthesis immediately after—e.g., Canadian International Development Agency (CIDA); thereafter use the abbreviation alone. Punctuate abbreviations with care. Omit periods in capitalized abbreviations, but include periods with lower-case abbreviations (see examples above).

6. Avoid contractions. Write "do not" instead of "don't"; "cannot" instead of "can't," etc. Your tone is thus more formal, a desirable effect in most essays.

7. Misuse of the possessive apostrophe is annoying. None of the personal pronouns needs an apostrophe. The word "it's" means either "it is" or "it has." The proper form of this possessive pronoun is "its."

8. The general rule is to add 's to the singular of *any* possessive noun (the cat's collar, Mr. Jones's house), but an apostrophe alone to the plural if it ends in *s* (the cats' collars, the Joneses' house). Plural nouns that do not end in *s* form the possessive by adding 's (children's).

9. The convention for using apostrophes with names ending in *s* is variable. Some writers will call an essay by George Williams "Williams' essay"; others, "Williams's essay." The latter is preferable since the former, read aloud, sounds like "William's essay"—which is wrong. If a possessive form sounds awkward aloud, consider using a prepositional phrase: instead of "Jesus's wisdom," write "the wisdom of Jesus."

10. Learn the basic rules of punctuation thoroughly. Whether it seems fair or not, grammar and punctuation—they are closely related—greatly influence your reader's response to your work. Faulty or irregular punctuation can be confusing, and may lead a reader to underestimate your ideas.

11. Bad spelling is distracting, and an otherwise good essay is likely to be penalized for it. Take responsibility for your spelling errors. Develop a list of words you are likely to misspell; review that list when you proofread your final draft. Use the spell-checker on your word processor, but do not rely on it alone (see item 5 on page 14). Buy a good dictionary and consult it whenever you doubt your spelling.

Avoiding Discriminatory Language

Nowadays readers, writers, publishers, and teachers are increasingly sensitive to evidences of bias in written language. As a courtesy to your reader, and as part of your social responsibility as a writer, you should avoid language that discriminates against other people with respect to their gender, race, social class, sexual orientation, and religious beliefs.

The English language contains a built-in bias in favour of males, but the convention that says "a person" is always "he" can readily be amended. In some cases, the phrase "he or she" may be substituted. Often a switch to the plural will circumvent the problem. You should adopt these and other similar usages including gender neutral nouns (e.g. "worker" instead of "workman," "flight attendant" instead of "stewardess") to ensure that you do not unwittingly offend your reader by an inappropriate choice of words.

Avoiding Plagiarism

Avoid plagiarism. It is a sort of literary sin a writer commits when using the words or ideas of another person without acknowledgment. The academic penalty for plagiarism, particularly the conscious, wilful kind, can be severe; but, beyond that, it is really a matter of personal integrity to give credit where credit is due.

A writer is guilty of plagiarism "when repeating or paraphrasing another's wording, when taking a particularly apt phrase, and when paraphrasing another's argument or presenting another's line of thinking" without full and proper acknowledgement (Gibaldi 71). Note the double quotation marks and documentation (author's name and page number) in the preceding sentence. You, too, must acknowledge, by means of such text references, your borrowing of someone else's words, ideas, data, or other information (even if you paraphrase or summarize rather than quote). Expressing someone else's idea in your own words does not make it yours. If you suspect you are plagiarizing, you probably are, as your instructor will soon recognize. Ironically, it is easier and more impressive to show off your well-chosen sources than to try to conceal them.

First-year students sometimes say, "But my whole essay is based on my reading. Does that mean every sentence must contain a parenthetical reference?" The short answer is "Yes"—if every sentence indeed contains a new and different source of material. But that is unlikely. Often a whole paragraph will draw upon one source, which can be acknowledged quite economically (see below for an example). Moreover, the beginning paragraph, setting out the thesis; the topic sentences and the conclusions drawn in the middle paragraphs; and the final, wider discussion in the ending paragraph, should all consist of the original words and ideas of the essay writer. Source materials, whether quoted, paraphrased, or summarized, have a supporting role, largely in the middle paragraphs. As the essay writer, you must be seen to be in charge of this material, selecting it, introducing it, organizing it, discussing it—and acknowledging it. See below for examples of what and what not to do.

Sample Source Material

The passage quoted below is taken from an essay by Cóilín Owens on the James Joyce short story "Araby," in a series anthology of literary essays on well-known stories. Approached carefully and critically, such essays can provide a useful stimulus as you begin your examination of a particular work. But they should *never* be a substitute for your own careful reading of the text and your own thinking; and they should *always* be properly acknowledged.

Read the passage, and then compare and contrast the two sample essay paragraphs that follow. The first plagiarizes the passage while the second acknowledges it properly.

> This is a story of the loss of innocence and the frustration of first love. The young boy's exaggerated expectations about the emotional rewards of his devotion to the little girl are cruelly deflated. He interprets the disappointing circumstances of his journey as a sign of the hollowness of the ideals with which he undertook that quest. He thus connects the frivolous banter among the young people and his own earlier brief conversation with Mangan's sister and thinks that he has perceived the banal reality behind the romantic image. Yet his perceptions in each case are unreliable: His immaturity causes him to overreact in each direction. The story, then, shows that the temptations to both the romantic inflation and to the cynical devaluation of experience are but two sides of the same false coin.[1]

---

1. Cóilín Owens, essay on "Araby," *Masterplots II: Short Story Series*, ed. Frank N. Magill, 10 vols. (Pasadena, CA: Salem, 1986) 107.

Plagiarized Version

Araby is a story about the loss of innocence and frustrated first love. The boy exaggerates his feelings for Mangan's sister and later they are deflated. He thinks the disappointments of his journey are a sign of the hollowness of his ideals when he went on his quest. Yet his ideas are unreliable and he overreacts. The story shows that romanticizing and devaluing experience are both false.

This short paragraph contains no acknowledgment whatsoever of the source of the ideas it presents; and it contains nothing original either. Owens's ideas are re-presented in simplified (sometimes oversimplified and distorted) form in the same order as they appear in the original passage. The writer does not challenge, discuss, or enlarge upon any key points. Some words and phrases are really quotations but are not acknowledged as such. (The short-story title lacks distinguishing quotation marks, as well.) The paragraph is inadequate in its paraphrase and incorrect as both paraphrase and quotation because acknowledgments are missing. It represents a common type of plagiarism, revealing a hapless dependency on an external source that the writer is probably too embarrassed to reveal. Now consider the following.

Properly Acknowledged Version

Cóilín Owens identifies a major theme of "Araby" in describing it as a story about "the loss of innocence and the frustration of first love" (107). The unfolding events show how the boy's romantic hopes are dashed when he sets out to prove his love for Mangan's sister on a journey Owens rightly refers to as a "quest." But Owens overlooks a key point in his assessment of what the boy's experience signifies. He says that the boy's "perceptions" are "unreliable," both in his "romantic inflation" of his feelings and in his later disillusionment (107). Yet the description of the sordid settings; of the careless indifference of the adults the boy encounters; and of the darkness, literal and figurative, in which he stands at the end, all derive from the perceptions of the adult narrator looking back at his younger self. The implication is that the boy learned a painful but truthful lesson about the society in which he was living.

There is room for disagreement about the interpretation offered here, but at least the source material is properly acknowledged and is used to develop an argument rather than just being silently appropriated. As an essay writer, you are not obliged to agree with the expert opinions you find expressed in your sources. You may, of course, use such opinions to lend authoritative support to your own. Here, however, the writer has taken a critic's opinion as a point of departure in order to develop a personal thesis .

Observe that the writer has introduced the source by name in the first sentence of the paragraph, and has supplied a page number in parentheses to indicate the location of the quotation, which is identified by double quotation marks. (The page number would also be required if the writer had paraphrased Owens instead of quoting him.) The short-story title is identified by double quotation marks, too.

Notice also that the source's name is introduced twice more, reminding the reader that a particular critic's views are being discussed. The original page number is reintroduced towards the end of the paragraph, and the reader understands that any intervening quotations or paraphrases are from the same page. (If intervening quotations or paraphrases were from different pages, additional parenthetical page numbers would be needed.) The final sentence, a conclusion drawn from the preceding discussion, expresses the essay writer's own ideas in the essay writer's own words. These ideas were developed in the context of expert opinion, quoted and paraphrased, and the process was opened up to the reader's view. The essay writer's own "voice" is heard throughout. By such straightforward means is plagiarism avoided. All that remains is to add the corresponding footnote or list of works cited.

~

Since paraphrase, summary, and quotation are vital components of essay writing, and since they are all susceptible to plagiarism, they deserve separate consideration.

Paraphrase
This term signifies the restatement of a short passage in other words.

Why Paraphrase?
1. You are more concerned with the original author's points than with the actual words—substance rather than style.
2. Too much quotation clutters the page; paraphrase provides variety, an alternative way of incorporating a source.
3. Your own expression, or "voice," should dominate the essay (very important).

How to Paraphrase
1. Use mainly short passages of paraphrase (one or two sentences), combining them with quotations and your own comments.
2. It is not acceptable to repeat the original and merely alter or cut a few words; instead, rephrase all the information *in your own words*.
3. Handle a key word, startling phrase, technical, or untranslatable term by quoting it.
4. Maintain a similar level of diction; the paraphrase should not be a watered-down version of the original.

You should paraphrase the more routine material in the original source, and quote only the most striking, significant statements. They will then stand out against a background of paraphrase. If you quote too much, the impact of individual quotations is weakened. You should therefore differentiate the more important statements (quotations) from the less important (paraphrases).

Summary

A summary is a condensation of a longer passage. A whole book could be summarized in a sentence, a chapter in a paragraph. The Owens passage quoted previously might be summarized as follows:

```
Owens claims that the young boy in "Araby" deceives
himself because he is too immature to understand the true
nature of his feelings for Mangan's sister.
```

This version is not only condensed but is expressed in language different from that of the original.

Quotation

The term *quotation* refers to your use of the *actual words* of another person, whether from a printed text, a lecture, an electronic source, etc. You must distinguish his or her words from your own by using quotation marks or other conventions (described below in "Quoting Effectively").

The presence of quotations, together with paraphrases and summaries, all accompanied by appropriate documentation, will lend credibility and the force of authority to the main points of your essay.

Often individual sentences will contain three kinds of language: your own words (introducing the topic, drawing conclusions, etc.), paraphrase or summary (source material expressed in your words), and direct quotation (taken word for word from the original). These three make a powerful combination.

Quoting Effectively

Often our reading inspires us to respond in writing; our ideas and expression are profoundly stimulated, guided, and even formed by the words of others. To invite the thought and language of other writers into our own work affirms our participation with other minds in the ceaseless effort to make sense of things. Our writing becomes more interesting and complex.

Purpose

In many courses, especially in the humanities and social sciences, the instructor expects your essays to reflect your reading. Quotations from respected authors in the discipline add variety and authority to your essay by introducing another voice or point of view, illustrating major points, and reinforcing your arguments. Find the strongest quotations you can—surprising details, vivid statements of controversy, prime examples, and insightful phrases and sentences that seem to condense a large idea into a memorable truth.

Note: since you have to provide references and corresponding citations for all quotations, it is essential that you make notes painstakingly when doing research. Use double quotation marks to distinguish quotations from paraphrase or summary; record the page number of each quotation (and paraphrased or summarized note); use ellipsis periods (see page 43) to indicate omissions in quotations.

How Much Quotation?

Avoid very long quotations, especially in a short essay. Quote only key passages. Make sure you know the desired balance between quotation and text. In English essays, usually 10-15 percent of the text is quotation, but a research essay or book report may require more. Ask your instructor. Excessive quotation suggests you are not doing enough of your own thinking; too little indicates you have not done the research.

References for Quotations (MLA Style)

If a word, phrase, or sentence deserves to be quoted, it also requires a reference. Provide a reference for *all* quotations, even brief ones. Typically, a reference includes an author's name and a page number. The name may appear in your sentence or in a parenthesis; the page number *always* appears in a parenthesis (see "References to Print Sources," on page 56; for APA style see "Text References," on page 92; for note style see page 102). When several successive quotations are taken from the same page, a single parenthesis after the last quotation of a series refers to all the quotations following the preceding reference.

Brief Quotations

Incorporate brief quotations—key words, phrases, or sentences—as smoothly as possible *within* your own sentences. Place double quotation marks around them:

```
Lawrence called the novel the "one bright book of life"
(126), elevating it above all other forms of literature.
```

Note: the quotation is a natural grammatical element of the sentence, needing only the quotation marks and the page number (the source, Lawrence, is already identified). Avoid using phrases such as "In the following quotation" or "as shown in this quote" since the quotation marks already indicate you are quoting.

A quotation can appear at the beginning, middle, or end of your sentence. Try to provide variety:

```
"The horror! The horror!"--this is Kurtz's last judgment
(608).
```

```
Atwood opposes any theory that limits expression: "Theory
is a positive force when it vitalizes and enables, but a
negative one when it is used to amputate and repress, to
create a batch of self-righteous rules and regulations"
(24).
```

Note: use a colon after a *complete* statement that introduces a quotation.

After phrases such as "so-and-so says," "she writes," "the report claims," "the law states," etc., which are not complete statements, use a comma to introduce the quotation that follows:

```
Vidal says, "of all writers, the one who does not mind
anonymity is the one most apt to appeal to an ambitious
[film] director" (139).
```

Omit this comma if you introduce the quotation with the word "that":

```
Vidal says that "of all writers, the one who does not mind
. . ." (139).
```

You may subordinate a quotation by placing it in a parenthesis. The page number is in *square brackets* to show a parenthesis within a parenthesis:

```
Ruskin answers the initial questions ("How does one define
children's literature?" and "How has the language of
children's literature changed?" [214]) with a good deal of
humour.
```

Use a pair of dashes, instead of parentheses or commas, as a way of emphasizing whatever is between them, including quoted material:

```
Ruskin is firm in her stand that many fairy tales,
nonsense poems, and folk legends--"originally intended for
an audience of any age at all" (215)--prove there is
continuity between childhood and adulthood.
```

Note: in the Courier font used for the essay examples throughout the *Style Sheet*, a dash is made from two hyphens, as on a typewriter. But in Times New Roman, you can create a full, single line dash—as in this example. In either case, do *not* insert letter spaces between the dash and the surrounding text.

Lengthy Quotations

Quotations that would comprise five or more lines of prose on your page should be distinguished visually from the rest of the text as a block. The *MLA Handbook* advocates the following: after one line space, begin on a new line, and indent the quotation one inch, or ten spaces, from the left margin. Double space the text of the quotation (see the example on page 29). If the quotation includes the first line of a paragraph, indent that line a further quarter inch, or three spaces, to indicate the paragraph break.

Do not use quotation marks around an indented block quotation unless they appear in the original source. In general, introduce such lengthy, and by implication important, quotations with a complete statement followed by a colon:

> While this movement in art was a rebellion against morbid, academic values, Ernst Fischer is critical of it:
>
>> Impressionism, dissolving the world of light, breaking it up into colours, recording it as a sequence of sensory perceptions, became more and more expressive of a very complex, very short-term subject-object relationship. The individual, reduced to loneliness, concentrating on himself, experiences the world as a set of nerve stimuli, impressions, and moods, as a "shimmering chaos," as "my" experience, "my" sensation. (71)
>
> In a world that is increasingly fragmented and dehumanized, the role of art as a force for achieving political awareness . . .

This example shows a complete statement, followed by a colon, introducing a lengthy, indented block quotation. Quotation marks appear only because they occur in Fischer's text. An additional indenting of a quarter of an inch, or three spaces, indicates Fischer's paragraphing. For indented block quotations, the parenthetical page reference goes *outside* the final sentence period after *one* letter space.

In some courses, for some instructors, you may be required to follow an older convention for presenting lengthy quotations. In this case, you leave a line space before and after the quotation which you *single space* and indent half an inch, or five spaces, from the left margin. Single spacing emphasizes the block format that is more in keeping with the design of printed books. If in doubt, ask your instructor which style you should use.

Common Faults

Do not try to make a quotation serve as the grammatical subject of a sentence (e.g., `"Art will disappear as life gains more equilibrium"` `proves what Mondrian means`). Do not insert space after opening or before closing quotation marks. Do not let a quotation stand on its own as an independent sentence; instead, introduce it with your own comment, perhaps mentioning the author's name. In every case, your own sentence must in some way surround the quotation, making it a coherent, natural part of your text. (Test whether or not a quotation fits by reading your whole sentence aloud, including the quotation.) Use quotations to back up your main points; do not quote unimportant matters of fact. A quotation should always *add* to the logical development of your discussion, not merely repeat it in different words.

Ellipsis

The ellipsis consists of three spaced periods . . . that indicate the omission of one or more words from a quotation. Do *not* put an ellipsis at the beginnings or ends of short quotations (single words or brief phrases), since they are self-evidently incomplete:

```
The book sets out to define "dehumanization" and what
Marcuse repeatedly calls the "one-dimensional man" (16).
```

Always use an ellipsis when you omit a word or words from *within* a quotation:

```
Lawrence states, "Freud is the starting point . . . in any
study of the mind" (78).
```

Also use an ellipsis: if a quoted fragment is reasonably lengthy; if it occurs at the end of your sentence; and if it lacks a period from the original quotation. In such a case, the order of items is: your words; beginning quotation marks; quotation; ellipsis; ending quotation marks; parenthetical page reference; and final period. If the quoted fragment ends with a period, the ellipsis is not needed.

```
Lawrence goes on to say, "Indeed, we find in Freud our
first true pioneer of the unconscious . . ." (80).
```

Leave a letter space between the last word of the quotation and the first period of the ellipsis.

Use an ellipsis to introduce a block quotation that does not begin with a sentence capital. An ellipsis is also necessary at the end of a block quotation which does not end with a period in the original; in this case, use four periods as shown below, with the page number set apart after one letter space:

```
In their introduction, Cunningham and Reich encourage us
to slow down, to become contemplative as we approach
artistic and literary works, because it would

        . . . help all of us to savor once again the power
        of language and image. That would be a great boon
        for ordinary life. It would enrich us, and . . .
        help us to be warily skeptical of the almost
        universal abuse of language and the shallowness of
        much of our artificial environment. . . . (3)
```

If you omit one or more sentences from *within* a quotation, use an ellipsis. A *complete sentence* of quotation must precede and follow the ellipsis, however. After the sentence period, place three spaced periods, leave another space, and continue with the balance of the quotation:

```
Thouless maintains that "We are allowing our brains to
degenerate into mere mechanisms when they were meant for
plasticity and change. . . . Inflexibility of mind would
lead to the extermination of the human race" (129).
```

Do *not*, however, use the three spaced periods to stitch together quotations from widely separated areas of the text. The effect is quite misleading. Link the quotations with your own words.

If you omit an entire line from a quoted block of poetry, insert in its place a line of spaced periods of approximately the same length:

```
In "The Far Field," as he contemplates eternity, Theodore
Roethke says:
```

```
        I learned not to fear infinity,
        The far field, the windy cliffs of forever,
        .  .  .  .  .  .  .  .  .  .  .  .  .  .  .  .  .  .
        The wheel turning away from itself,
        The sprawl of the wave,
        The on-coming water. (51-52, 53-55)
```

Note: line numbers are provided here in a parenthesis one letter space after the end of the quotation.

Brackets

Use square brackets when you must alter, or add, a word or phrase within a quotation to make the quotation fit grammatically, or to supply a proper name to a pronoun lacking a clear antecedent:

```
The same critic writes, "When we first meet him [Hamlet],
a spirit of gloom prevails . . ." (41).
```

Use this device only when you have to. Almost any sentence can be rewritten to incorporate the quotation as it originally appears, or the quotation can be trimmed to eliminate the offending word or phrase:

```
The same critic writes that when the audience first
encounters Hamlet, "a spirit of gloom prevails" (41).
```

Errors in Quotations

Occasionally you may come across a serious factual or style error, or a spelling mistake, in a quotation you plan to use. If you wish to draw attention to the error, place the Latin word "sic" (meaning "thus") in square brackets after it, as in the following example:

```
According to J. N. Sullivan, "At the time of writing Moby
Dick [sic] the problem that was to haunt Melville was, as
it were, fairly straightforward" (15).
```

The reader will understand that the errors in the title *Moby-Dick* (the lack of italics and a hyphen) occurred in the original source.

Quotation Within a Quotation

In block quotations, preserve quotation marks exactly as they appear in the original—do not supply marks of your own. But when you incorporate a short quotation into your sentence, and any part of that quotation contains double quotation marks, change them to *single* ones.

Original:

> Hopkins's invention of what he called "sprung rhythm," "instress," and "in-scape" provided a sense of liberation to early twentieth-century poets.

Your sentence:

```
Ezra Pound is one of many poets who found "a sense of
liberation" in "Hopkins's invention of what he called
'sprung rhythm,' 'instress,' and 'inscape'" (Markham 61).
```

Generally, your quotation marks take precedence over the original ones. In the above example, you are quoting both Markham and Hopkins, and so you need both double and single marks to distinguish between the original authors.

Stated as a rule: when you are quoting any one author, use double quotation marks. Use single quotation marks only if a second author intervenes. Note, too, that quotation marks appear around each individual word and phrase in the series quoted above. They are not lumped together as "sprung rhythm, instress, and inscape" because they do not appear together that way in the original source.

Special Use of Quotation Marks

Quotation marks can indicate your ironic use of someone else's term. You may use such marks (sparingly) to stand for a phrase like "so-called":

```
The shelves were stocked with "natural" food products.
```

Punctuating the Close of Quotations

All punctuation that appears immediately before your closing quotation marks must be grammatical. Thus you do not always have to quote the writer's punctuation, but instead may sometimes supply your own. Your period or comma should go *inside* the quotation marks, unless a parenthetical reference is necessary, in which case your punctuation follows the parenthesis. You should retain the author's question mark or exclamation mark, but not the author's colon, semicolon, or dash, when they appear at the end of a quotation.

Original:

> ... they are wise and aware; they enjoy life with gusto, yet face and accept death; they not only work productively but creatively, and they obviously love their fellow human beings ...

Your sentence:

```
The author admires people who are "wise and aware," who
"enjoy life with gusto," and who "accept death"; to him
truly sane people function "productively" and
"creatively"; most importantly, they "love their fellow
human beings" (Peck 125).
```

Original:

> Are we to consider individuals healthy simply because they are not in pain—no matter how much havoc and harm they bring to their fellow human beings?

Your sentence:

```
Peck asks, "Are we to consider individuals healthy . . .
no matter how much havoc and harm they bring to their
fellow human beings?" (125).
```

Your sentence:

```
Can we trust Peck's analysis of "how much harm they [evil
people] bring to their fellow human beings" (125)?
```

Note: your punctuation takes precedence over the original. In the example immediately above, your question mark rules the sentence, not Peck's.

Italics Appearing in Quotations (MLA Style)

Any word, phrase, or complete sentence that appears in italics in the original source should be underlined in your quotation (but see item 4 on page 14).

Original:

To start at the end first, *the peak-experience is only good and desirable, and is never experienced as evil or undesirable.*

Your sentence:

```
Maslow begins by claiming that "peak-experience is only
good and desirable" (76).
```

Note: if you wish to draw your reader's attention to a word or phrase in a quotation, you may underline it, but only if you include a special phrase in acknowledgment:

```
Daily life, to Lawrence, is merely a facade; the true life
is actually to be found in the "subterranean regions of
the soul" and in the "primitive" conscious life of the
body (94, emphasis added).
```

Quoting Poetry

Incorporate a line or part of a line of poetry as though you were quoting prose. For example,

```
Williams's poem is about "how to perform a funeral."
```

Page and line numbers are unnecessary when you quote from short poems. Simply acknowledge the source in your sentence or in a content note (see "Content Notes" on page 25).

For a quotation of two or three lines, indicate line endings with a slash:

```
From the start, Williams's poem is didactic, promising
some kind of ethical lesson: "I will teach you my
townspeople / how to perform a funeral."
```

Leave a letter space before and after the slash. Note that there is no slash at the beginning or end of the quotation. To indicate a stanza break, use a pair of slashes // without a letter space between them.

When you quote more than three lines, use *block* form, indented one inch or ten spaces from the left margin:

```
One passage in particular demonstrates his individual
sense of rhythm:

        To you
            I can risk words about this
        Mastering them you know
            they are dull
                servants
        Who say less
            and worse
                than we feel
```

In a block quotation, try to duplicate the layout of the original poem as closely as possible, imitating the poet's margins, spacing, punctuation, and any peculiarities of typography.

Long lines of poetry require special treatment in block form. To make more room, indent the first line half an inch or five spaces and run it to the right margin; indent the overflow on your next line(s) a further quarter of an inch or three spaces. What you have shown as two or more lines will thus be understood to be a single line in the original.

Quoting Drama

For brief drama quotations, treat prose dialogue as if it were from a short story or novel, and introduce the name of the character in your sentence. In block quotations of dialogue, indent one inch or ten spaces as usual. Begin with the speaker's name, followed by a colon and the dialogue. Omit any stage directions unless pertinent.

```
The relationship is characterized by constant tension and
bickering:

        Charley: Don't get insulted.
        Willy: Don't insult me.
        Charley: I don't see no sense in it. . . . (43)
```

For verse drama, follow the convention for references described in "References to Classic Literary Works," page 59.

THE MLA STYLE
OF DOCUMENTATION

Whenever you quote other people's actual words, paraphrase or summarize their ideas, or make use of their data or original information, MLA style requires that you acknowledge your indebtedness by means of references in your text keyed to a corresponding list of works cited (see "Works Cited" on page 62). Together these two forms of documentation are sufficient for your readers to appreciate the variety and quality of your sources, and to locate them for the purposes of their own research.

Purpose of References

Provide text references (see below for examples) either *within your sentences*, or *in parentheses*, or in combination:

1. to indicate the source, including page number(s) for printed materials, of any quotation you include in your text;
2. to acknowledge your indebtedness for factual information and for ideas paraphrased, or summarized (i.e. not directly quoted), from any source;
3. and to direct readers to the list of works cited for complete details of publication.

Content of References to Print Sources

A text reference to a print source usually contains the following:

1. the last name of the author—*either* in your sentence, *or* as the first item in a parenthesis that follows any quotation, paraphrase, or summary you used;
2. the title of the work, *either* in your sentence, *or* in a parenthesis—*if* you have referred to *more than one work* by the same author;
3. the page number(s) *in a parenthesis* for any quotation, paraphrase, or summary you used.

The content of a parenthetical reference usually takes one of the three following forms:

(87) page number alone; you have already identified the author in your sentence

(Breit 87) author's last name (no punctuation following) and page number; you have *not* identified the author in your sentence

`(Breit, `<u>`Writer`</u>` 87)` author's last name, comma, title (abbreviated from *The Writer Observed*, a book, hence underlined) and page number; you included the title to distinguish it from another work by the same author that you have also referred to in your essay

With few exceptions (the Bible, an encyclopedia, a dictionary, or a one-page article), every parenthetical reference to a print source will contain a page number. Do not mention page numbers elsewhere in your sentences.

For anonymous works, the title (usually abbreviated) replaces the author's name in the parenthesis.

Remember, the parenthesis should *not* repeat details already given in your sentence.

References in Sentences or in Parentheses?

You have a choice: include references either in the body of your sentences or in parentheses. This flexibility allows you to achieve different effects:

1. `Einstein and Infeld introduce their history of modern physics as though they were fiction writers: "In imagination there exists the perfect mystery story" (`<u>`Evolution`</u>` 3).`

   This sentence emphasizes the *authors* rather than the source. The inclusion of the abbreviated title in the parenthesis indicates that more than one work by these authors has been referred to, and reveals the specific source of the quotation.

2. `In `<u>`The Evolution of Physics`</u>`, a layman's guide to physics from Galileo to quantum mechanics and relativity theory, Einstein and Infeld distinguish between Arthur Conan Doyle's and their own "detective novel" (4).`

Although it mentions the authors, this sentence draws attention to the work suggesting that it is central to the discussion.

3. Few would argue with the theory that "Human thought
   creates an ever-changing picture of the universe"
   (Einstein and Infeld 9).

Here the sentence is more concerned with the *idea* than with the source; thus the authors are subordinated in the parenthesis.

4. Some modern physicists (e.g., Einstein and Infeld)
   approach their discipline as though it were a creative art
   or a special branch of philosophy.

Since Einstein and Infeld are just two among many, their names are subordinated, and because nothing has been quoted, paraphrased, or summarized, there is no page number.

The point is that the content of your reference may vary according to what element you wish to stress in the sentence.

Placement of Parentheses

In the majority of cases, it is appropriate to place the parenthesis at the end of the sentence in which the reference (quotation, paraphrase, or summary) occurs. It goes *inside* your period but *outside* any ending quotation marks:

Like most authorities, Zinsser emphasizes that unity is
one of the bases of effective writing (46).

According to Zinsser, unity satisfies the reader's
"subconscious need for order" (46).

Sometimes, however, you may end the reference part way through the sentence and then introduce a new reference or a comment of your own. In such cases, you should place the parenthesis inside the punctuation at the end of the clause in which the reference appears:

```
Unity is one of the bases of effective writing (Zinsser
46); it is not, however, easy to achieve.
```

If you refer to an author in passing, then place the parenthesis immediately after his or her name, again inside any adjacent punctuation:

```
Most authorities, including Zinsser (46) and Strunk and
White (6), emphasize that unity is one of the bases of
effective writing.
```

When you use a block quotation, place the parenthesis *one* letter space after the final period:

```
            You learn to write by writing. It is a truism
            worn thin by repetition, but it is still true.
            . . . The only way to learn to write is to
            force yourself to produce a certain number of
            words on a regular basis. (Zinsser 45)
```

The question often arises of what to do with several references occurring in quick succession. Must every clause or sentence contain a parenthesis? Not necessarily. By pulling together research material from the same page of a particular source, you can reference a whole paragraph of text by using an author's name, accompanied by a page number in parentheses, in a sentence at the beginning of the paragraph together with another page number in parentheses towards the end. The reader understands that all the intervening material appears on the page referred to.

In a lengthy paragraph, you can remind your reader about your source by reintroducing the author's name or by using an appropriate pronoun, perhaps in conjunction with a quotation (for which, of course, you must provide a parenthetical page number). See "Properly Acknowledged Version," beginning on page 35, for an example.

If you refer to material from several different pages, then you must introduce the various page numbers in parentheses. And if you have referred to several different authorities, their names must appear, too. But often, as suggested above, you will be able to economize on the number of parentheses you use by consolidating your research material.

References to Print Sources

○ **AUTHOR'S NAME AND TITLE IN TEXT**
(you referred to entire work so no page number, no parenthesis)

```
William Zinsser's On Writing Well provides a wealth of
good advice about writing.
```

Note: for a first reference in your sentence, you may use an author's full name as given on the title page, e.g., William Zinsser. Subsequently, the last name alone will suffice, i.e., Zinsser.

○ **AUTHOR'S NAME IN TEXT WITH PAGE NUMBER IN PARENTHESIS**
(you did not refer to another work by same author)

```
As Zinsser has said, "Unity is the anchor of good writing"
(46).
```

Note: for a first reference in your sentence, you may use an author's full name as given on the title page, e.g., William Zinsser. Subsequently, the last name alone will suffice, i.e., Zinsser.

○ **AUTHOR'S NAME IN TEXT WITH ABBREVIATED TITLE IN PARENTHESIS**
(you referred to another work by same author)

```
As Zinsser has said, "Unity is the anchor of good writing"
(Writing 46).
```

○ **AUTHOR'S NAME NOT IN TEXT** (so last name in parenthesis)

```
The beginning writer should always be aware that "Unity is
the anchor of good writing" (Zinsser 46).
```

○ **AUTHOR'S NAME AND ABBREVIATED TITLE IN PARENTHESIS**
(you referred to another work by the same author)

The beginning writer should always be aware that "Unity is the anchor of good writing" (Zinsser, Writing 46).

○ **TWO OR THREE AUTHORS CITED IN PARENTHESIS**

The purely visual impact of writing deserves attention: "paragraphing calls for a good eye as well as a logical mind" (Strunk and White 12).

○ **MORE THAN THREE AUTHORS CITED IN TEXT**

Lauer et al. discuss ten points that are important in the writing process (2-3).

Note: "et al." is an abbreviation for the Latin *et alii*, meaning "and others."

○ **MORE THAN THREE AUTHORS CITED IN PARENTHESIS**

At least ten points are important in the writing process (Lauer et al. 2-3).

○ **REFERENCE TO AN INDIRECT SOURCE**
(original author mentioned in text)

According to R. D. Laing, "true sanity" requires "the dissolution of the normal ego, that false self competently adjusted to our alienated social reality . . ." (qtd. in Roszak 50).

Note: you discovered the quotation from Laing in a work by Roszak, and you wish to use part of it. As shown here, you must acknowledge both authors. The phrase "qtd. in"—the abbreviation for "quoted in"—indicates that your reader can locate the complete Laing quotation by looking under

"Roszak" in your works cited. Do not provide an entry under "Laing" unless he is your direct source elsewhere in the essay. If, however, you think the original source may be of special interest to your reader, document it in a content note (see page 25). If you had paraphrased Laing's idea instead of quoting him, the parenthesis would still contain "qtd. in."

○ **REFERENCE TO AN INDIRECT SOURCE**
(original author not mentioned in text so included in parenthesis)

```
We are told that "true sanity" requires "the dissolution
of the normal ego, that false self competently adjusted to
our alienated social reality . . ." (Laing, qtd. in Roszak
50).
```

○ **REFERENCE TO AN UNSIGNED ARTICLE**

```
In the southern part of the Selkirk Mountains lie "vast
areas of both igneous rocks of Mesozoic age and very
complex metamorphics" ("Selkirk").
```

Note: whenever your source does not provide the author's name, use an abbreviated version of the title. Here "Selkirk" corresponds to the word under which the work is alphabetized in works cited. No page number appears because the article is alphabetized in an encyclopedia, making the reference easily traceable. If the article appears in a periodical or newspaper, provide a page number.

○ **REPEATED REFERENCE TO ONE OR TWO WORKS**
When you quote and/or paraphrase from *one* source (a novel, essay, etc.), give a *full footnote for the first reference* (see "The Note Style of Documentation" beginning on page 101), using an arabic superscript number in your text and a full-sized number in your footnote. Add to this footnote a short sentence directing the reader to the text references:

```
1. F. Scott Fitzgerald, The Great Gatsby (New York:
```

```
Scribner's, 1925) 23. Subsequent page references are also
to this edition.
```

Thus your text will contain references showing page numbers only, as in the following example. No works-cited page is necessary since all of the information your reader needs is present in the footnote.

```
Although Nick sees that Tom and Daisy are responsible for
much of Gatsby's tragedy, he seems unable to censure them
completely, realizing that "what he [Tom] had done was, to
him, entirely justified . . ." (180).
```

If you refer repeatedly to only *two* sources, provide two footnote references. This situation may arise in essays that compare or contrast. Your reader must, however, know clearly from your text which source you are referring to; to avoid confusion, include an author's name or a title in your sentence, or an author's name in your parenthesis.

If you use more than two sources, follow the regular conventions for text references, and provide a list of works cited.

References to Classic Literary Works

For some literary works, additional details may be required in the reference. For works of classic prose literature available in different editions, you should provide a chapter number, and a book number when relevant, in addition to the page number. Give the page number first; then, after a semicolon, give the extra detail(s) using abbreviations ("bk." for "book," "ch." for "chapter"):

```
In Tom Jones, Fielding humorously defends his right to
ransack the works of ancient authors without either
acknowledgment or scruple (474-75; bk. 12, ch. 1).
```

Use arabic numerals instead of roman. In the above example, "XII" in the edition cited converts into "12." Note, too, that a comma goes between the book and chapter references.

For classic poems and verse plays, you should omit page numbers; instead, provide division numbers—i.e., the number of any book, canto, part, act, or scene—together with the line numbers:

```
                    Give me that man
    That is not passion's slave, and I will wear him
    In my heart's core, ay, in my heart of heart,
    As I do thee. (Ham. 3.2.67-70)
```

Note: in a parenthesis, though *not in the text*, the titles of famous works may be abbreviated: thus "Hamlet" becomes "Ham." In an essay exclusively on this play, however, where the source of the quotation is clear, it is not necessary to include the title in the parenthesis. In the above block quotation, "3" is the act number; "2" is the scene number; and "67-70" are the line numbers. Use arabic numerals and use periods without spaces to separate them. Do not signify lines by using the letters "l" or "ll."

References to the Bible or Other Sacred Texts
Unless you indicate otherwise, your reader will assume you are using the King James Version of the Bible, or the standard versions of other sacred works:

```
    Few know that after the resurrection Jesus stayed with his
    disciples for forty days, "speaking of the things
    pertaining to the kingdom of God" (Acts 1.3).
```

Note: underlining, page numbers, and works-cited entry are not required. Here "1" is the chapter number and "3" is the verse number.

References to Media Sources
When you acknowledge a media source by a reference in your sentence, you eliminate the need for a parenthesis, since no page number is involved. You may include both a name (of an author, film director, radio or television artist, musician, etc.) and a title (of a play, film, radio or television program, record album, CD, audiocassette, CD-ROM, etc.), as in the following:

```
    In Citizen Kane, Orson Welles created a virtual
    encyclopedia of film technique.
```

Note: since the emphasis is on the director, his name should precede the title of the film in the list of works cited (see page 81).

Of course, a parenthesis containing a name or a title *will* be required for the acknowledgment of facts, information, and ideas from a source not introduced in your sentence (CBC Radio, in the following example):

<u>Bizarre Books</u>, soon to be published by Macmillan, is a bizarre book listing and describing some of the bizarrest works ever to appear on a hopeful bookseller's shelves (<u>As It Happens</u>).

References to Internet Sources
In some cases, references to Internet sources will be identical in form to references to print sources. An author's, editor's, or compiler's name (or, lacking these, a title) will appear in your sentence, or in a parenthesis accompanied by a page number, *if the source is paginated*. But often you will find that an Internet source is not paginated: in effect the work is one long page. Section or paragraph numbers may be given instead of page numbers, in which case include them in the parenthesis after the appropriate abbreviation: "sec." for "section" and "par." for "paragraph."

If no number of any kind is given, then you need no parenthesis (assuming the author is referred to in your sentence). To assist your reader, however, you could count down to the particular paragraph (or section and paragraph) containing your reference material and give that number in a parenthesis. A conscientious reader will have the same counting to do, too, but that is easier than scanning a whole article. A parenthetical paragraph reference will look like this:

In "Hoop Dreams," Sarah Banet-Weiser argues that "women's professional basketball has been defined as a cultural arena that is primarily about gender" (par. 5).

See page 85 for the corresponding works-cited entry for this reference and for further advice on online pagination problems.

References to Government Sources
If the identifying name for a government citation is short, e.g., "Bill C-9," then

you may place it in the parenthesis together with the page number. But if additional lengthy details are needed, they are better introduced in your sentence:

```
According to the Final Report of the Royal Commission on
Bilingualism and Biculturalism, . . . (Canada 131).
```

Works Cited

The works-cited page should list *every* source you actually used in your text and for which you provided a text reference (do not fabricate a list of vaguely pertinent works you did not directly refer to). In the text-referencing system, this list is the sole provider of publishing (or broadcasting) details.

Print Sources
For book details, refer to the title page and the copyright page (the reverse of the title page), *not the cover.* Make a note of the title in full (including subtitle), the author(s), the publisher, the city of publication, the year of publication, and the page number(s) for each reference. Other details should be recorded if present: editor(s); translator; author of foreword, afterword, preface, or introduction (only if named on the title page); edition and volume numbers; and article, essay, story, and poem titles from collections, together with inclusive page numbers for the *whole* item.

Government Sources
Record the name of the government, or jurisdiction, responsible for the publication, plus the name of any relevant department, agency, office, committee, or other subdivision of the government structure. Also record titles and, where relevant, volume numbers and full dates (day, month, year), the government publisher, and the date of publication. See pages 75-79 for examples.

Media Sources
Record details from introductory radio announcements, television, film, and CD-ROM credits; and from the liner notes accompanying long-playing record albums (LPs), compact discs (CDs), laser discs, digital video discs (DVDs), computer diskettes, audio- and videocassettes, and audiotapes (reel to reel).

Include names of directors, performers, presenters, creative artists, etc., as appropriate, plus titles; album, disc, and tape numbers; radio and television station and network names; album, disc, and tape distributors; and dates of broadcast, release, or distribution. For a work of art, record the name of the artist, the title of the work, and the name of the institution and city where the work is housed.

Internet Sources

For an Internet source, record the author's name; the title of the document; its publishing history if it was originally a printed work; the date it was posted online (or revised); the date you accessed it; and the network address or uniform resource locator (URL) found in the address window of your browser. Be sure to get it exactly right: the directory path of a URL is case-sensitive, so don't switch a capital letter to lower case, or vice-versa. Also record the name of any online subscription service you may have used, and the location at which you accessed it (see example on page 85). If given, record inclusive page numbers, or the total number of sections or paragraphs, for online articles and documents. See "References to Internet Sources," on page 61, and "Article Accessed through an Online Service," on page 85, for further advice on dealing with online pagination or the lack thereof. For electronic mail, record the writer's name, the name of the person receiving the e-mail, its title or subject line, and its date.

$\sim$

Remember that only some of these details go into your text references, while others are reserved for works cited. Save unnecessary rechecking of sources by writing down *full* citations as you do your research.

Preparing the Works-Cited List

Follow these rules as you prepare your list:

1. Centre the words Works Cited half an inch below the page number. The list always appears as the last page(s) of the essay.
2. Number each page of works cited, continuing the numbering of the text. The numbering on the sample works-cited page (see page 89) follows MLA

research-essay style with the page number accompanied by the writer's last name in a running headline. As an alternative, depending on your instructor's wishes and the kind of essay you are writing, you may use the page number alone either centred or placed against the right margin half an inch from the top of the page.

3. The text reference (usually an author's name) *must match* the entry in works cited (which usually begins with an author's alphabetized last name).

4. Do not subdivide the list into categories unless asked to by your instructor.

5. Begin the first line of each entry at the left margin (see sample, page 89); indent subsequent lines of that entry by half an inch or five spaces.

6. Double space each entry, and double space between entries.

7. Do *not* number the entries.

8. List entries *alphabetically* by the *last name* of the first author (or director, performer, creative artist, etc.) mentioned in the work's publishing or broadcasting information. For radio and television programs, films, and other media sources, you may begin the entry with the title of the work, rather than a name, depending on the emphasis you wish to give (see examples, beginning on page 80).

9. When no author is given, alphabetize the entry by the first word in the title. Disregard "A," "An," or "The," but leave the article in its usual place.

10. Capitalize the first and last words in the title (and subtitle, if any), and all the principal words. Do *not* capitalize articles, prepositions, coordinating conjunctions, or the "to" in infinitives. Separate a title and a subtitle with a colon.

11. Underline the title (and subtitle) of a separately published work; put quotation marks around short-story, short-poem, article, and essay titles.

12. For books, give the first city of publication listed on the title page or copyright page. To the name of an unfamiliar city, add an identifying detail: the abbreviated name of a US state, Canadian province, or English county, etc.

13. Use a shortened form of a publisher's name. Give only the first name, if more than one appears, and omit "Co.," "Inc.," etc. Use "Harper," rather than "Harper and Row Inc." or "HarperCollins." Use "UP" (no periods) for

"University Press." See pages 272-274 of the *MLA Handbook* for a list of abbreviations of publishers' names.

14. For books, give the year of publication recorded on the title page or on the copyright page after the symbol © (but do *not* include this symbol). Give the last *edition* date, but ignore reprint dates. If no date is given, write "n.d."

15. For daily and weekly publications, give the full date (day, month, year) of issue; for monthly publications give the month and year.

16. For films, CDs, LPs, audio- and videocassettes, CD-ROMs, computer diskettes, and other media, give the year of release or issue. Give the full date (day, month, year) for radio and television broadcasts, and interviews.

17. For most media sources, state the medium of publication before the name of the manufacturer or distributor. See pages 80-83 for further details and examples.

18. The key item in an Internet citation is the URL or Internet address; be sure to get it *exactly* right. Depending on your material, you may need to include three dates: the year of publication of your source's original print version; the full date (day, month, year) on which the Internet version was posted (or revised); and the full date on which you accessed the source on your computer. See pages 84-87 for further details and examples.

19. Do *not* give page numbers unless you are citing an article in a journal, periodical, or newspaper, or an item in a collection (a short story, essay, or poem, etc.). Then give the page numbers of the *whole* article or item.

20. *Punctuate each entry carefully.* The sample works-cited page (page 89) and the model entries below indicate the conventions for punctuating citations. Use a period followed by *one* letter space after each major division in a citation. Use a comma between an author's last and first names, and between the publisher's name and the year of publication, but use a colon after the city of publication.

Sample Citations

The list of works cited should employ the same conventions of indentation, order of items, use of underlining or quotation marks, punctuation, abbreviation, etc., illustrated below and on the sample page. Most of the types of sources you are likely to use are exemplified. *To cite a source, find a corresponding example from the entries that follow, and imitate the style.* If you can find no suitable model, consult Chapter 5 of the *MLA Handbook*.

Print Sources

○ BOOK WITH ONE AUTHOR

```
Bruder, Mary Newton. Much Ado About a Lot: How to Mind
     Your Manners in Print and in Person. New York:
     Hyperion, 2000.
```

Note: leave one letter space after each major section of your citation, as shown throughout these examples.

○ TWO OR MORE BOOKS BY THE SAME AUTHOR

```
Parker, John F. The Independent Writer. Fort Worth, TX:
     HBJ Coll. Pubs., 1986.

---. Writing: Processed Product. Evanston, IL: MacDougal,
     1991.
```

Note: to indicate the repeated name, place three hyphens at the left margin followed by a period. If the name refers to an editor or translator, then place a comma after the hyphens followed by the appropriate abbreviation, e.g., `---, ed.`

○ BOOK WITH TWO OR THREE AUTHORS

```
Strunk, Jr., William, and E. B. White. The Elements of
     Style. New York: Macmillan, 1972.
```

Note: for the purpose of alphabetizing, the first author's name is reversed (with commas after both names); subsequent names appear in their usual order.

BOOK WITH MORE THAN THREE AUTHORS

Lauer, Janice M., et al. Four Worlds of Writing. 2nd ed.
    New York: Harper, 1985.

BOOK WITH AUTHOR AND EDITOR (you have quoted the author)

Freud, Sigmund. A General Selection from the Works of
    Sigmund Freud. Ed. John Rickman. Garden City, NY:
    Anchor-Doubleday, 1957.

Note: when citing the name of a publisher's special imprint—e.g., "Anchor"—give the imprint name first, followed by a hyphen and the publisher's name.

BOOK WITH AUTHOR AND EDITOR
(you have quoted the editor's preface)

Rickman, John, ed. Preface. A General Selection from the
    Works of Sigmund Freud. By Sigmund Freud. Garden
    City, NY: Anchor-Doubleday, 1957.

BOOK IN TRANSLATION

Camus, Albert. "The Myth of Sisyphus" and Other Essays.
    Trans. Justin O'Brien. New York: Vintage, 1955.

BOOK WITH FOREWORD BY ANOTHER AUTHOR
(you have quoted the foreword)

McCourt, Frank. Foreword. Eats, Shoots & Leaves: The Zero
    Tolerance Approach to Punctuation. By Lynne Truss.
    New York: Gotham, 2004.

Note: McCourt's name begins this citation because you quoted his foreword. Note, too, that "Foreword" appears in full after his name, followed by a period, and that the word "By" precedes the name of the author. Follow the same style when you quote from an introduction, preface or afterword by another author.

○ **BOOK WITHOUT AUTHOR OR EDITOR**

The National Geographic Atlas of the World. 7th ed.
    Washington: Natl. Geog., 1999.

Note: this citation would be alphabetized by title under the letter "N" in the works cited without regard to "The."

○ **BOOK WITH CORPORATE AUTHOR**
(committee, corporation, council, association, etc.)

Council on Economic Priorities. Star Wars: The Economic
    Fallout. Cambridge, MA: Ballinger, 1987.

Note: "MA" is the abbreviation for Massachusetts. (See pages 264-65 of the *MLA Handbook* for a list of abbreviations of geographical names.)

○ **BOOK WITH EDITION STATEMENT**

Zinsser, William. On Writing Well: An Informal Guide to
    Writing Nonfiction. 4th ed. New York: Harper, 1990.

○ **BOOK IN A SERIES**

Parr, Richard T. A Bibliography of the Athapaskan
    Languages. National Museum of Man Mercury Series,
    Ethnology Service Papers 14. Ottawa: National Museums
    of Canada, 1974.

Note: sometimes a publisher produces several volumes in the same format, dealing with the same general area of research. Each book has its own title but belongs to a series. Include the name of the series and the number in the series if they are indicated, as in the example above. Underline the book title, but not the series name.

○ **REPUBLISHED BOOK**

Collin, W. E. <u>The White Savannahs</u>. Introd. Germaine
    Warkentin. 1936. Toronto: U of Toronto P, 1975.

Note: this book was originally published in 1936. It went out of print and then was republished in 1975. The date of original publication is therefore given immediately before the publishing details for the republished edition. The abbreviation "U" stands for "University," and "P" stands for "Press."

○ **ANTHOLOGY OR COLLECTION** (you have cited the editors)

Cone, Edward T., Joseph Frank, and Edmund Keeley, eds. <u>The</u>
    <u>Legacy of R. P. Blackmur: Essays, Memoirs, Texts</u>. New
    York: Ecco, 1987.

Note: the colon here, and in "Book With Edition Statement" above, introduces a subtitle. The subtitle often appears only on the title page, and is sometimes distinguished by a different typeface, but nonetheless you must include it in the full title in works cited.

○ **STORY IN AN ANTHOLOGY**

Tyler, Anne. "Holding Things Together." <u>We Are the Stories</u>
    <u>We Tell: The Best Short Stories by North American</u>
    <u>Women Since 1945</u>. Ed. Wendy Martin. New York:
    Pantheon, 1990. 150-63.

Note: when citing a story or essay in an anthology, or a magazine, journal or newspaper article, give inclusive page numbers for the whole piece (e.g. "150-63" above). Where single numbers appear in the examples below, the pieces comprised one page or less.

○ ESSAY IN AN ANTHOLOGY

Guth, Alan. "A Golden Age of Cosmology." The New
    Humanists: Science at the Edge. Ed. John Brockman.
    New York: Barnes, 2003. 285-96.

○ POEM IN A MULTIVOLUME ANTHOLOGY

Rossetti, Christina. "An Apple Gathering." 1861. The
    Norton Anthology of English Literature. Ed. M. H.
    Abrams et al. 4th ed. Vol. 2. New York: Norton, 1979.

Note: you may include the original date of publication followed by a period, after the title. If you used both volumes of this work, put the number of the volume you referred to into the parenthetical text reference separated from the page number(s) by a colon: (2: 1522-23). If you used one volume, give the volume number in the citation only (e.g. "Vol. 2" above).

○ TWO OR MORE WORKS IN AN ANTHOLOGY

Barkley, Jacqueline. "Reclaiming our Children: Teachers as
    Elders." Neilsen 183-93.

Milne, Marlene. "Bending the Willows." Neilsen 65-79.

Neilsen, Allan R., ed. Daily Meaning: Counternarratives of
    Teachers' Work. Mill Bay, BC: Bendall, 1999.

Note: to avoid repetition of publishing details when citing two or more different works in an anthology, list the anthology separately. For individual works referred to in your text, give the author's name, and the title, followed by the editor's last name and the inclusive page numbers for the whole piece. Thus the name "Neilsen" in the first two entries above provides a cross reference to the last entry, which contains the full publishing details. The names of the authors and editor are listed alphabetically in works cited, in the usual way.

REVIEW OF A FILM, PLAY, BOOK, EXHIBITION, ETC.

```
Corliss, Richard.  "A Vampire With Heart." Rev. of Bram
    Stoker's Dracula, dir. by Francis Ford Coppola. Time
    30 Nov. 1992: 69.
```

Note: the abbreviation "dir." for "directed" indicates that a film review is being cited—"by" alone would signify a book review. Here Corliss is the reviewer, and "Rev. of" stands for "Review of." Observe that there is no punctuation between the magazine title and the date, but that a colon, followed by one letter space, goes between the year and the page number. For weekly magazines, the date replaces the volume number, and so is not enclosed in parentheses.

ARTICLE IN A JOURNAL WITH A VOLUME NUMBER

```
Meier, Kathryn S. "Tobacco Truths: The Impact of Role
    Models on Children's Attitudes Toward Smoking."
    Health Education Quarterly 18.2 (Summer 1991):
    173-82.
```

Note: journals are scholarly publications appearing monthly, quarterly, or yearly. Magazines usually appear weekly or monthly and are more widely available, often at newsstands. The term "volume" refers to the collection of issues in an annual series.

If a journal begins each new issue with page 1, add a period and the issue number immediately after the volume number—in the example above, 18 is the volume number, and 2 is the issue number. Some libraries shelve journals by date rather than by number, so it is helpful to include the month (or season) and year in a parenthesis, as shown.

If a journal uses an issue number but not a volume number, include it as if it were the volume number.

If a journal has continuous pagination throughout the volume, i.e., does not begin each issue with page 1, give the volume number followed by the year of publication in a parenthesis, a colon, and the inclusive page numbers of the article you cited, as in the following example.

Rau, Santha Rama. "Benares: India's City of Light."
    National Geographic 169 (1986): 215-51.

○ ARTICLE IN A WEEKLY OR MONTHLY MAGAZINE

"Nanotechnology: The Next Small Thing." Economist
    17-23 Jan. 2004: 52.

Note: no author's name is given, so begin the citation with the title.

Thomas, Lewis. "On the AIDS Problem." Discover May 1983:
    42+.

Note: the + sign in the above citation shows that the article begins on page 42 but is then interrupted by intervening material. For frequently published magazines, indicate the issue by date alone; omit volume and issue numbers.

○ ARTICLE IN A NEWSPAPER (no author's name given)

"The Problem: How to Fill Pension Piggybank." Vancouver
    Sun 18 Jan. 2000: A18.

Note: many newspapers paginate by section. In this case provide both section and page, without a space between. When a newspaper is paginated continuously, give the page number(s) alone.

○ ARTICLE IN A NEWSPAPER (author's name given)

Clarke, Jack. "Learning the Lessons of War." Province
    7 Mar. 1999: 41.

○ ARTICLE IN A REFERENCE WORK (no author's name given)

"San Bernardino Mountains." Encyclopedia Americana.
    1991 ed.

Note: begin with the article title when no author is given. Because encyclopedias usually arrange articles alphabetically throughout, volume and page numbers are omitted. If the work is well known, specify only the edition, if stated, and the year of publication. For less-well-known reference works, give full publishing details (see below).

○ **ARTICLE IN A REFERENCE WORK**
(author's name and full publishing details given)

```
Brock, Dan W. "Public Policy and Bioethics." Encyclopedia
    of Bioethics. Ed. Warren T. Reich. Rev. ed. 5 vols.
    New York: Simon-Macmillan, 1995.
```

Note: pages are numbered consecutively throughout all five volumes, so there is no need to specify a particular volume here—the page numbers in your parenthetical text reference will suffice. "Simon-Macmillan" abbreviates and combines the names Simon and Schuster and Macmillan.

○ **ARTICLE REPRINTED IN A REFERENCE WORK** (author's name given)

```
Thomas, Clara. "The Wild Garden and the Manawaka World."
    Modern Fiction Studies 22 (Autumn 1976): 401-12.
    Excpt. and rpt. in Contemporary Literary Criticism.
    Ed. Dedria Bryfonski. Vol. 13. Detroit: Gale, 1980.
    342-44.
```

Note: you referred to excerpts from Clara Thomas's previously published article (only parts of which are reprinted in your source). You give the original source first, and then the source you used. "Excpt." and "rpt." are abbreviations for "excerpted" and "reprinted." If the whole article was reprinted, you would use "Rpt." only. You include page numbers for the whole Clara Thomas section.

○ **INTRODUCTION IN A REFERENCE WORK**

```
"(Adeline) Virginia Woolf." Introduction. Twentieth-
    Century Literary Criticism. Ed. Sharon K. Hall.
    Vol. 5. Detroit: Gale, 1981. 505-06.
```

Note: here you begin with the title of the whole section on Woolf. You include "Introduction" because you referred to it and not the excerpts that follow it—no author is given. Because the series alphabetizes within each volume and not throughout, you give the volume number. You also include the page numbers for the introduction because it is only part of the section on Woolf.

YEARBOOK, ANNUAL

Canadian Global Almanac 2005. Toronto: Wiley, 2005.

CONFERENCE PROCEEDINGS

Second National Forum on Handgun Control: Proceedings.
7-9 Jan. 1976. Washington: United States Conference
of Mayors, 1976.

ANNUAL REPORT

International Joint Commission. Annual Report on Great
Lakes Water Quality. Windsor, ON, 1978.

Great Britain. Colonial Office. Annual Report on the
Social and Economic Progress of the People of Hong
Kong. London, 1938.

SPECIAL REPORT

City of Vancouver Task Force on Atmospheric Change. Clouds
of Change: Final Report. Vancouver, 1990.

PAMPHLET

Acid Rain. Society for Promoting Environmental
Conservation (SPEC), n.d.

Note: sometimes pamphlets omit essential details, as here. No author is given or date of publication, hence the abbreviation "n.d." for "no date." But as far as possible, cite a pamphlet as if it were a book.

○ COURSE WARE

Lau, Evelyn. "More and More." English 1121 Reader:
    Selected Essays and Nonfiction. Comp. Pybus. 4th ed.
    Vancouver: Langara College, 2004. 27-38.

Note: some academic institutions publish photocopied course ware (sometimes referred to as "course packs") in-house under licence from Access Copyright to serve the needs of particular courses. Here "Pybus (first name not given) is the compiler of the material. Sometimes the compiled material is repaginated; sometimes the original pagination is preserved. Cite whatever page numbers are available.

○ RESERVE ARTICLE

Roberts, James D. Catholics, Divorce and Remarriage.
    Photocopy of text of a lecture to the conference of
    the Assn. of Separated and Divorced Catholics,
    Toronto, 19 Sept. 1986. Revised 1989. Placed on
    reserve at Langara College Library, Vancouver.

Note: items placed on reserve are often published books or journal articles. In such cases, cite them in the normal manner, with full publishing details.

Government Sources

Citations for government-issued documents and publications usually begin with the jurisdiction, or government name, which stands in place of an author's name. This may be followed by the relevant department, agency, office, committee, or other subdivision of the government structure. If an author's name is given, it is introduced with "By" immediately following the title (see "Government Publication," below).

PARLIAMENTARY DEBATE

```
Canada. Parliament. House of Commons. Debates. Official
     Report. 33rd Parliament. 2nd session. Vol. 14,
     6 July-17 Aug., 1988. Ottawa: Queen's Printer, 1990.

British Columbia. Legislative Assembly. Debates. Official
     Report. (Hansard.) 34th Parliament. 3rd session. Vol
     15, 6 July-20 July, 1989. Victoria: Queen's Printer,
     1990.
```

Note: "Queen's Printer" is the publisher-of-record for many older federal government documents. Nowadays the official publisher for the Government of Canada is Canadian Government Publishing. In the US, the United States Government Printing Office (GPO), publishes the *Congressional Record* and thousands of federal government documents.

CONGRESSIONAL DEBATE

```
United States. Congress. Senate. Senator Kerry of
     Massachusetts speaking for the International Dolphins
     Conservation Act of 1992, H.R. 5419. 102nd Cong., 2nd
     sess., Congressional Record (8 Oct. 1992), vol. 138,
     no. 144. Daily ed.
```

Note: the *Congressional Record*, published by the GPO, is the official transcript of all the proceedings of both houses of Congress. It appears first in a daily edition; a revised edition is published later in bound volumes and other formats. Be sure to cite the daily edition if it is your source because its pagination is different from the final version. If your essay text provides enough detail and context, a shorter citation with page numbers may be sufficient. The style shown below is recommended by the *MLA Handbook*. If in doubt, consult your instructor.

```
Cong. Rec. 8 Oct. 1992: S17840-S17843.
```

COMMITTEE REPORT

Canada. Parliament. House of Commons. Standing Committee
on National Health and Welfare. Report on AIDS in
Canada. Ottawa: Queen's Printer, 1986.

United States. Congress. House. Select Committee on Aging.
Subcommittee on Health and Long-term Care. Elder
Abuse: A National Disgrace. A report by Rep. Claude
Pepper, subcommittee chair. 99th Cong., 1st sess.
Committee print. Washington: GPO, 1985.

STATUTE

Canada. Competition Act, R.S.C. 1985, c. C-34, as am. by
R.S.C. 1985, c. 19 (2nd Supp.), s. 19 [formerly the
Combines Investigation Act].

Note: the citation for an act, or a section of an act, is presumed to include the
amendments to it. You would list amendments only if you had specifically
referred to them. "R.S.C." stands for "Revised Statutes of Canada"; C-34 is
the chapter number; "am." is the abbreviation for "amended," "c." is for
"chapter" and "s." is for "section."

British Columbia. Education Excellence Appropriation
Repeal Act, S.B.C. 1988, c. 10.

Note: "S.B.C." stands for "Statutes of British Columbia."

STATUTE

Iraq Sanctions Act of 1990. Statutes At Large. Vol. 104,
part 3, sec. 586 (1990). Washington: GPO, 1990.

Note: once passed into law, bills and joint resolutions are called statutes, and
are published by the GPO in annual editions of Statutes At Large. Statutes
also become part of the United States Code, which the GPO updates and

publishes at six-year intervals. The code is organized by "title," with sections within each title. A short-form citation begins with the title number but is alphabetized under "United States Code." A more detailed form of citation, including statute name, may be preferred. Samples of both follow. Choose one style and be consistent.

```
42 US Code. Secs. 7401-7641. 1988.

Clean Air Act. United States Code. Title 42, secs.
    7401-7641 (Vol. 17, 1988). Washington: GPO, 1988.
```

○ BILL

```
Bill C-9, An Act to Facilitate Combatting the Laundering
    of Proceeds of Crime. 34th Parliament. 3rd session,
    1991. (Second Reading, 20 June 1991.)
```

Note: the "C" for "Commons"—House of—in the bill number indicates the jurisdiction. Bills originating in the Senate bear an "S." Since bills are numbered from 1 in each parliament, include the parliament number, the session, the sessional year(s), the reading, and the reading date. Do the same for provincial bills.

```
Bill 90, Property Rights Act. 34th Parliament. 4th
    session, BC, 1991. (Second Reading, 21 Mar. 1991.)
```

Note: for provincial bills, begin with the bill number and include the jurisdiction following the session number.

```
United States. Congress. Senate. Aviation Security
    Improvement Act. 101st Cong., 2nd sess., HR 5732.
    Congressional Record. Vol. 136, no. 146. Daily ed.
    (23 Oct. 1990), S16544-S16551.
```

Note: bills and resolutions are numbered alphanumerically. Above, "HR 5732" indicates a bill originating in the House of Representatives. "S" would indicate the Senate; "S. Res." means Senate Resolution, and so forth.

○ BY-LAW

City of Vancouver. <u>Downtown Office Development Plan</u>.
    (Adopted by By-Law No. 4912, 4 Nov. 1975.)

○ GOVERNMENT PUBLICATION (author or editor given)

United States. Dept. of State. <u>The United States and</u>
    <u>Russia: The Beginning of Relations, 1765-1815</u>. Ed.
    Nina N. Bashkina, et al. Washington: GPO, 1980.

Note: use "By" instead of "Ed." when an author's name is given. Or, you may begin the citation with the name of the author or editor. Better still, cross reference the item by author or editor name, as below:

Bashkina, Nina N., et al., eds. 1980. See US. Dept. of
    State. 1980.

○ CONGRESSIONAL COMMITTEE HEARING

United States. Congress. Senate. Committee on the
    Judiciary. <u>The Constitutional Roles of Congress and</u>
    <u>the President in Declaring and Waging War: Hearings</u>
    <u>Before the Committee on the Judiciary</u>. 102nd Cong.,
    1st sess., 8 Jan. 1991. Washington: GPO, 1991.

○ ROYAL COMMISSION REPORT

Canada. Royal Commission on Bilingualism and
    Biculturalism. <u>Final Report</u>. 6 vols. Ottawa: Queen's
    Printer, 1967-1970.

○ **TREATY**

> United States. Dept. of State. "Treaty Between the United
>   States of America and the Union of Soviet Socialist
>   Republics on the Limitation of Anti-Ballistic Missile
>   Systems," 26 May 1972. TIAS no. 7503. United States
>   Treaties and Other International Agreements, vol. 23,
>   pt. 4.

Note: "TIAS" stands for "Treaties and other International Acts," a series of State Department pamphlets which are compiled and published by the GPO in the above-cited reference work.

Media Sources

For audio- and videocassettes, audiotapes, LPs, DVDs, laser discs, slide programs, film strips, microforms, computer diskettes, CD-ROMs, and interviews, state the medium (before the name of the manufacturer or distributor where applicable). Naming the medium is not required for radio and television programs, CDs, films, and works of art.

○ **RADIO PROGRAM**

> Enright, Michael. "The Enright Files." Ideas. Host Paul
>   Kennedy. CBC Radio. CBU, Vancouver. 6 June 2005.

Note: CBC Radio is the network; CBU is the local broadcast station.

○ **TELEVISION PROGRAM**

> Cat On a Hot Tin Roof. By Tennessee Williams. Dir. Jack
>   Hofiss. American Playhouse. PBS. KCTS/9, Seattle. 31
>   July 1985.

Note: the series title, American Playhouse, appears after the program reference, and is not underlined or put in quotation marks. PBS is the network, and KCTS/9 is the broadcast station.

○ **FILM**

```
Welles, Orson, dir. Citizen Kane. With Welles and Joseph
    Cotten. RKO, 1941.
```

Note: Welles and Cotten are identified as principal actors. Other individuals may be mentioned when relevant to your text, e.g., producer, screenwriter, film score composer, etc. If you have emphasized the film rather than the director in your text, the title should appear first with the director's name following.

○ **AUDIO RECORDING** (LP, CD, audiocassette, audiotape)

```
Sainte-Marie, Buffy. "Eagle Man/Changing Woman." Up Where
    We Belong. EMI Music Canada, 1996.
```

```
Ellington, Duke. "A Tone Parallel to Harlem (The Harlem
    Suite)." 1951. Uptown. Audiocassette. CBS, n.d.
```

Note: for LPs (but not CDs), audiocassettes, and audiotapes, the medium appears *before* the distributor's name. The above audiocassette is a re-release of previously recorded material. The cassette's liner notes indicate 1951 as the original recording date. No date is given for the issue of this cassette, hence "n.d." If a date is given, include it.

○ **VIDEO RECORDING** (videocassette, DVD, laser disc)

```
The Human Experiment. Ethics in America Series 9.
    Videocassette. Intellimation, 1989.
```

Note: for videocassettes, DVDs, or laser discs, the medium again appears before the distributor's name.

○ **SLIDE PROGRAM**

```
Learning by All Means. Slide program. Media and Library
    Association and California Audio Visual Education
    Distributors Association, n.d.
```

○ FILMSTRIP

Michelangelo: The Sistine Chapel. Filmstrip. Life
    Filmstrips, 1950.

○ WORK OF ART

Van Gogh, Vincent. Starry Night. Museum of Modern Art, New
    York.

Note: underline the title of a sculpture, a painting, or any other "published" work of art.

○ MICROFORM (microfilm, microfiche, microprint, etc.)

Richardson, Penelope L. "Issues in Television-centered
    Instruction." Proceedings of the Annual Meeting of
    the American Educational Research Association, Los
    Angeles, Apr. 1981. ERIC Document Reproduction
    Services ED20521 (1981).

Note: give details for the original published source (underlined) of the work cited; then give the name (also underlined) of the microform source you actually used, followed by the volume number and the year (in parentheses). Put a colon instead of a period after the date and add fiche and grid numbers if they will assist the reader to locate the relevant material.

○ CD-ROM

"Abolitionist Movement." Compton's Interactive
    Encyclopedia. CD-ROM. N.p.: Compton's New Media,
    1994.

Note: in this example, an encyclopedia article, no author is given and "N.p." indicates that no place (i.e. city) of publication is given. If known, the author's name would precede the title in the normal fashion.

○ INTERVIEW

```
Prince, Linda. Personal interview. 2 Aug. 2003.
```

Note: begin with the interviewee's name and then state the type of interview, i.e. whether it is personal (face to face), by telephone, or by e-mail. Then add a period and follow with the interview date.

In general, an interview has weight only when you are citing an authority—someone with informed opinions. Indicate his or her credentials in your text:

```
College librarian Linda Prince said that. . . .
```

Interviews published in newspapers and magazines, or broadcast via radio and television are identified as to type by the publishing or broadcasting details you provide. Begin with the interviewee's name followed by the name of the interviewer (after "Interview with"), if given; if not given, just use "Interview." Include the title, if any, underlined if the interview is separately published or broadcast; in quotation marks if part of a larger work.

```
Bowering, George. Interview with Rebecca Wigod. "Canada's
      First Poet Laureate Turns the Page." Vancouver Sun 14
      May 2005.

Keating, Brian. Interview with Rick Cluff. The Early
      Edition. CBC Radio One. CBU. Vancouver. 21 June 2005.
```

○ SPEECH or LECTURE

```
Carr, Shirley. "The Trade Union Outlook on Serious
      Concerns of the 1990s and Beyond." Empire Club of
      Canada. Royal York Hotel, Toronto. 15 Mar. 1990.
```

Note: if there is no title, indicate the type of oral presentation given, e.g., speech, lecture, reading, etc. Do not underline this designation or put it in quotation marks.

Classroom lectures may be cited in similar style. Give the lecturer's name, the title of the lecture, if any ("Lecture," if not), the course name, the name of the institution and the city in which it is located, and the date the lecture was given.

Internet Sources

For information on the publishing details required for Internet works-cited entries, see "Internet Sources," on page 63, and "References to Internet Sources," on page 61. Follow the order of items set out in the sample entries below.

Some specific Internet pages have long, complex URLs containing unusual characters. If you encounter one, omit the directory path and give only the URL of the Web site's home page, i.e., the protocol (http or ftp, etc.) and host name down to the first back slash. Let your reader follow the appropriate links from there. That way you reduce the risk of transcription errors. (See also "Government Document Online" below.)

○ **ARTICLE IN A JOURNAL ONLINE**

```
Zuga, Karen F. "Addressing Women's Ways of Knowing to
     Improve the Technology Environment for All Students."
     Journal of Technology Education. 10.2 (Spring 1999):
     57-71. 3 Feb. 2000 <http:// scholar.lib.vt.edu/
     ejournals/JTE/v10n2/zuga.html>.
```

Note: this journal is published in both print and electronic versions, so the larger part of this entry follows the style for a printed article: author, article title (in quotation marks), journal title (underlined), volume and issue numbers (10.2), date of publication (in parentheses), and inclusive page numbers (57-71). What follows is specific to the online version: the date you accessed the article (3 Feb. 2000), and the URL (network address) enclosed in angle brackets. If the URL runs on to another line, break it after a slash. Here the URL (which contains volume and issue numbers) will take your reader directly to your source.

○ ARTICLE IN A MAGAZINE ONLINE

```
Davis, L. J. "Medscam: A Mother Jones Investigation."

     Mother Jones Magazine Mar.-Apr. 1995. 1 Dec. 1999

     <http://www.mojones.com/mother_jones/MA95/

     davis.html>.
```

Note: the magazine article cited above is from a "full text archive," but there is no reference to the print-version page numbers. If you wish to access the entire issue of the magazine, rather than just this article, make "MA95/" the last item in the URL.

○ ARTICLE ACCESSED THROUGH AN ONLINE SERVICE

```
Banet-Weiser, Sarah. "Hoop Dreams." Journal of Sport and

     Social Issues 23.4 (Nov. 1999): 403. 18 pp. Online.

     Academic Search Elite. EBSCOhost. Langara Coll. Lib.,

     Vancouver. 18 Jan. 2000.
```

Note: "EBSCOhost" is the name of the online service that publishes the database called "Academic Search Elite" (underlined). The Langara College Library is included because it subscribes to the service and provides access to students. "Online" identifies the medium; if the medium is obvious (e.g., a URL appears) omit it. You accessed the article on 18 Jan. 2000.

Some databases give page numbers as they appear in the original print version of an article. In this case, only the number of the first page (403) and the total number of pages (18) were given.

When you print an article from a database, your copy's page numbers may not correspond to the original page numbers. To direct your reader to the precise location of your reference material, count paragraphs (or paragraphs within a section) and give the appropriate paragraph (and, if necessary, section) number.

PRINTED BOOK ONLINE

Austen, Jane. <u>Pride and Prejudice</u>. [1813] New York:

    Scholastic, 1962. 17 May 2005

    <http://austen.thefreelibrary.com/

    Pride-and-Prejudice>.

Note: the date of first publication is given in brackets after the title, followed by publishing details for the specific edition posted online. This unadorned text (the illustrations for this edition are omitted) is available free, together with background information on the author and a separate selection of links to useful Web sites.

WEB SITE

<u>College Writing Programs</u>. UC Berkeley, 2002. 3 June 2005

    <http://www-writing.berkeley.edu/>.

Note: often a Web site will identify an editor, or compiler, or even a curator. If so, give the name after the title. "UC Berkeley" is the sponsor of the site.

WEB DOCUMENT

Tyner, Ross. <u>Sink or Swim: Internet Search Tools and

    Techniques</u>. Vers. 5. Rev. Ross Tyner and Walter

    Slaney. Spring 2001. Okanagan UC. 9 Sept.2003

    <http://www.ouc.bc.ca/libr/connect96/search.htm>.

Note: "Tyner" is the author of the document which he later revised with the help of "Walter Slaney." "Vers. 5" is the version number; "Spring 2001" is when the document was posted on the Web site; "Okanagan UC" ("University College") is the sponsor; "9 Sept. 2003" is the date the document was accessed.

○ SECTION OF A WEB PUBLICATION

Ross, David P., and Paul Roberts. "Family Income and
   Children's Development." Income and Child Well-Being:
   A New Perspective on the Poverty Debate. N.d.
   Canadian Council on Social Development. 14 Apr.2005
   <http://www.ccsd.ca/ pubs/inckids/1.htm>.

Note: "Family Income and Children's Development" is one section among several in *Income and Child Well-Being*.

○ GOVERNMENT DOCUMENT ONLINE

Canada. Statistics Canada. "Population Reporting on
   Aboriginal Identity, by Age Group, by Provinces and
   Territories, 2001 Census." 22 Mar. 2005
   <http://www40.statcan.ca/>.

Note: the URL for this document page is subject to constant change and yields only a "File not found" message if used. So just give the URL for the Statistics Canada home page, where a search tool will locate the required data.

○ ELECTRONIC MAIL

Sawyer, Don. "Tomorrow Is School." E-mail to Raymond
   Bendall. 22 Jan. 2000.

Note: use the message's "Subject" heading as a title if the message is not titled in any other way. If no title or subject is present, the citation is shortened to:

Sawyer, Don. E-mail to Raymond Bendall. 22 Jan. 2000.

○ WEBLOG

"Google Scholar." Internet Scout Project Weblog. U of

Wisconsin, Madison. 22 Nov. 2004. 14 June 2005

<http://scout.wisc.edu/Weblog/>.

Note: this Weblog provides a constantly updated and wide-ranging list of interesting, sometimes quirky, topics selected by academics as a byproduct of their Net searches. Be sure to include the date of posting which is prominently displayed on each listing.

Sample Works-Cited Page (MLA Style)

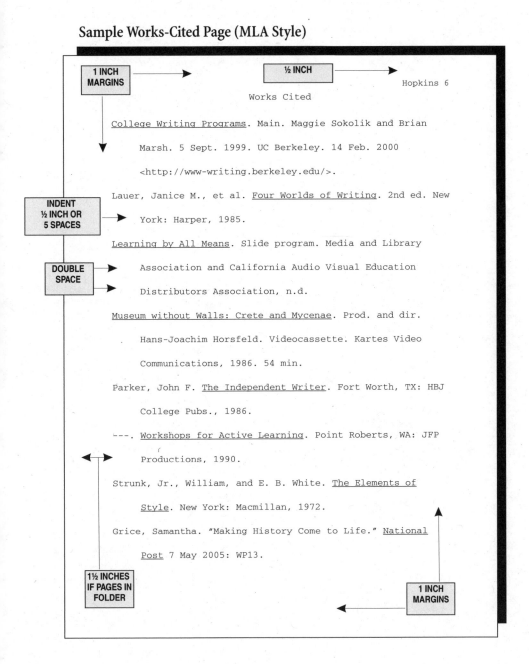

1 INCH MARGINS

½ INCH

Hopkins 6

Works Cited

College Writing Programs. Main. Maggie Sokolik and Brian

Marsh. 5 Sept. 1999. UC Berkeley. 14 Feb. 2000

<http://www-writing.berkeley.edu/>.

Lauer, Janice M., et al. Four Worlds of Writing. 2nd ed. New

INDENT ½ INCH OR 5 SPACES

York: Harper, 1985.

Learning by All Means. Slide program. Media and Library

DOUBLE SPACE

Association and California Audio Visual Education

Distributors Association, n.d.

Museum without Walls: Crete and Mycenae. Prod. and dir.

Hans-Joachim Horsfeld. Videocassette. Kartes Video

Communications, 1986. 54 min.

Parker, John F. The Independent Writer. Fort Worth, TX: HBJ

College Pubs., 1986.

---. Workshops for Active Learning. Point Roberts, WA: JFP

Productions, 1990.

Strunk, Jr., William, and E. B. White. The Elements of

Style. New York: Macmillan, 1972.

Grice, Samantha. "Making History Come to Life." National

Post 7 May 2005: WP13.

1½ INCHES IF PAGES IN FOLDER

1 INCH MARGINS

THE APA STYLE OF DOCUMENTATION

The influential American Psychological Association (APA) advocates a style of documentation, usually referred to as the author-date system, both for indicating sources of quotations, paraphrases, and summaries, in the text of an essay, and for listing references at the end. APA style is designed for writers who intend to publish their papers. The advice that follows is therefore adapted to meet the needs of college students. With minor variations, the social sciences (Psychology, Anthropology, and Sociology) and some physical sciences (e.g., Biology) employ the APA conventions outlined here.

Below is a sample page from a long article that was accepted for publication. It illustrates several major features of APA style including page format, a variety of typical references for paraphrase and summary, and the use of direct quotations. The writer used APA software that will paginate, print running heads, and help build a proper list of bibliographic citations. Student essays may not require page headings. Consult your instructor.

Page Format

1. For your title page you may use a layout similar to that in the sample on page 27. Although it does not correspond in all respects to APA publication style, it is suitable for college-level essays. APA convention requires that essay titles appear in upper- and lower-case letters and not in all capitals (check the rules for capitalization in item 10 on page 64).

2. A running head appears flush right in the upper right corner of every page, including the title page, a half inch from the top. The heading includes the essay title, if brief, or a shortened form of a long title, followed by five spaces, and then the page number.

3. Leave one-inch margins around the text on each page.

Text References

1. Parenthetical references do not contain titles.

2. When you quote an author whose name is in your sentence, provide the date in parentheses immediately after the name, and a page reference

(using "p." or "pp.") directly after the quotation and before the sentence period. (See the last sentence of the first paragraph of the sample page.)

3. When you quote without indicating the author in your text, the reference after the quotation is as follows:

```
" . . . narrative revisions" (Webster, 1991, p. 65).
```

4. When you use paraphrase or summary and refer to the author in your sentence, the parenthesis contains only the date of publication. Page numbers are not required in the parenthesis for paraphrased or summarized material.

5. When you use paraphrase or summary without mentioning the author in the sentence, your reference should include the last name (no initials) of the author(s), followed by a comma, and the date (see next item).

6. Use an ampersand (&) instead of "and" for two authors in a parenthetical reference: (Webster & Young, 1988).

7. If two or more works by the same author were published in the same year, distinguish between them by coding each with lower-case "a," "b," "c," etc., in order of their appearance in your list of references:

```
Bonanno (1988b) proposes that the true . . .
```

8. If a work has three, four, or five authors, include all their last names (no initials) in a first reference. In subsequent references, include the last name of the first author followed by "et al." (no italics). Use this latter style for all references, including the first, if a work has six authors or more.

9. If more than one source has contributed to the content of a summary or paraphrase, arrange them in alphabetical order by author; include the dates, and use a semicolon to separate them:

```
(Bruner, 1986; Spence, 1984)
```

Using Notes in APA Style

Content or informational notes use the same numbering convention as for MLA note style (see page 25). The notes are double-spaced under the head -

ing `Footnotes` on a separate page following the references page. Indent the first line of each note five spaces from the left margin.

Bibliographic Citations

In the APA style of documentation, the list of bibliographic citations is headed `References`. In preparing your list, follow the guidelines set out below.

APA style requires that the titles of separately published works (books, periodicals, microfilm publications, etc.), foreign words, and some technical terms (see page 100 of the APA *Publication Manual*) be italicized. If you have a problem meeting this requirement, consult your instructor.

1. Begin a fresh page (continuing the pagination of the text) by centring the word `References` half an inch below the running head.
2. Begin the first line of each entry at the left margin (see sample page 100) and indent subsequent lines five spaces.
3. Double-space throughout the list.
4. For more than one author, all names and initials appear in reverse order (not just the first); give all last names in full, but all first names in initials only; use "&" instead of "and" before the last name.
5. List two or more works by the same author(s) in chronological order (earliest publication first), spelling out the author's last name and initials in each entry.
6. Place a period after each major part of an entry.
7. Following the name(s) of the author(s), place the year of publication in a parenthesis—hence the term "author-date" system.
8. If you have used two or more works published in the same year by the same author or co-authors, code the dates in succession with "a" then "b" then "c," and so on.
9. Next comes the title of the book or article. For a book, italicize the title and subtitle, and capitalize only the first word of the title and subtitle, except for proper names. For an article, do *not* use quotation marks, and capitalize as for a book title.
10. The city of publication and the name of the publisher, linked by a colon, precede the final period (e.g., second model entry). The names of publish-

ers, including university presses, are spelled out in full (but omit "Co.," "Ltd.," etc., as well as articles and initials).

11. The name of a journal, using upper- and lower-case letters, is italicized. A comma separates it from the volume number (in arabic numerals, without "vol."), which is also italicized (e.g., last entry).

12. If volumes of a journal are numbered continuously, provide inclusive page numbers for the article, without "pp." (e.g., last entry).

13. If each issue in a volume is numbered separately, include the issue number in a parenthesis following the volume number (e.g., first entry).

14. If the article is from an edited collection or anthology (not a periodical), the word "In" introduces the names of the editor(s), followed by "ed." or "eds." plus a comma, and then the book title (italicized). Inclusive page numbers follow directly in a parenthesis (no punctuation precedes), with "pp." to indicate "pages" (e.g., third entry).

15. For journal articles online, first give the publishing details for the print version: author(s), date of publication (in parentheses), article title, journal title and volume number (italicized), issue number if needed (in parentheses), and inclusive page numbers, followed by a period. Then write "Retrieved" followed by the date you accessed the article, and the source. Put a colon after a Web site name that introduces a URL. Omit the colon if the URL is the sole source (e.g., next to last entry). Do not enclose the URL in angle brackets, MLA style, but omit the final sentence period to avoid confusion (e.g., next to last entry).

Documenting Research in Sociology

The American Sociological Association (ASA) *Style Guide* employs an author-date system similar to that of the APA, so consult the previous section when preparing your Sociology essays. Some of the differences between the two styles are noted below.

Text References

1. Do not put a comma after the last name(s) of the author(s) in the parenthetical reference.
2. Include page numbers (without "p." or "pp.") for direct quotations and detailed text references (see below).
3. Put a colon between the page numbers and the year:

   ```
   (Giddens 1987: 15); (Giddens 1979c: 37-38)
   ```

4. For block quotations, indent the text five spaces and single space.

Bibliographic Citations

1. Invert the name and initials of the first author only.
2. Do not put the year of publication in parentheses; instead, put a period after the name(s) of the author(s) .
3. Use "p." or "pp" with the inclusive page numbers when citing a whole magazine article, or a chapter of a book, but not when the page numbers are accompanied by a volume or issue number: e.g., "27: 182-84."
4. Enclose URLs in parentheses.

Documenting Research in Biology

Biology essays use APA conventions, with some exceptions:

Text References

1. For two authors, use "and" not "&" in the parenthesis:

   ```
   (Smith and Jones, 1991).
   ```

2. Place a comma after the author(s).
3. Quotations are generally not used.
4. If you must quote or indicate a specific page from a book, the page number follows the date and a colon, without "p." or "pp.":

   ```
   The Indole test was performed to isolate Salmonella from
   Edwardsiella (Barnett, 1988: 380); a negative result
   ```

confirmed `Salmonella.`

5. As shown above, references usually appear inside your sentences, as close as possible to the material you have used.
6. In order to show that several consecutive pieces of information in your paragraph have the same source, place the reference at the end, after the sentence period:

```
. . . and confirmed that Salmonella usually produces
hydrogen sulfide. (Sneath, 1984: 415)
```

Note: in both references and citations, Latin names for species are italicized.

Bibliographic Citations

1. The list may be headed either `Literature Cited` or `References`.
2. Include names of all authors, spelling out the last names only and using initials for first and middle names.
3. Following the author(s) comes the year of publication, standing alone without parentheses.
4. Write out the complete title of an article, without quotation marks and capitalizing only the first word:

```
Singer, S. J., and G. Nicholson. 1972. Fluid mosaic model
        of the structure of cell membranes. Science 175: 720.
```

5. Abbreviate complex journal names but not one-word names.
6. Following the volume number (without "vol.") of a journal, a colon precedes the inclusive page numbers given in full:

```
Marine Biol. 85: 157-166.
```

7. For book titles, indicate volume number, if any (use "Vol."), publishing information, and pages consulted (use "pp."). The publisher precedes the city with a comma between them.

Laskin, A. I., and H. A. Lechevalier, eds. 1973. *CRC Handbook of Systematic Microbiology*. Vol. 2. Williams and Williams, Baltimore, MD., pp. 118-124.

Sample Text Page (APA Style)

1 INCH MARGINS

In terms of the clinical/reminiscence domain there has been an emerging emphasis on the distinction between "historical truth" and "narrative truth" (Bruner, 1986; Spence, 1984). The former connotes a static reservoir of directly (although not necessarily easily) retrievable and unimpeachable "facts"; the latter explicitly acknowledges the reconstructive and dynamic nature of memory recall and is more concerned with its verisimilitude than with documentable accuracy. Within the parameters of narrative truth, clinicians and clients jointly facilitate the retrieval and elucidation of memories which form a life portrait supported by current self-structures (e.g., Webster & Young, 1988). This is a dynamic process leading to narrative revisions, defined by Bonanno (1990) as "the re-evaluation or re-experiencing of the past in the context of a new conceptual framework" (p. 176).

In terms of autobiographical memories, McAdams (1989) demonstrated that personality factors (i.e., themes of intimacy and power) were strongly associated with autobiographical memories of "peak experiences." Specifically, themes of intimacy or power were higher in peak experience protocols of subjects who had correspondingly high themes on prior projective personality measures such as the Thematic Apperception test.

In the area of mood-memory congruency (Blaney, 1986;

1 INCH MARGINS

Sample References (APA Style)

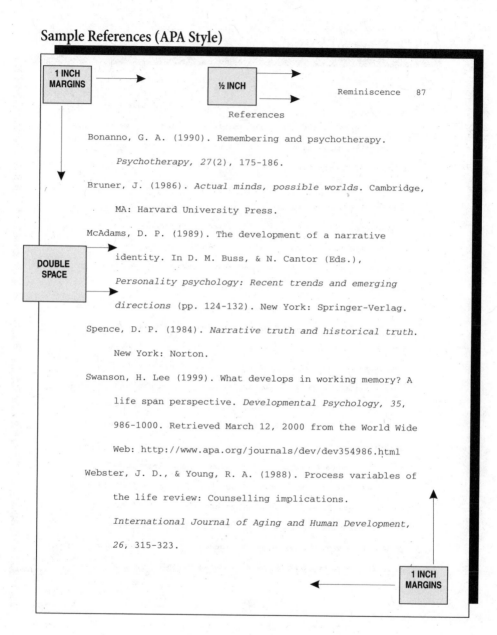

1 INCH MARGINS

½ INCH

References

Bonanno, G. A. (1990). Remembering and psychotherapy.

    Psychotherapy, 27(2), 175-186.

Bruner, J. (1986). *Actual minds, possible worlds*. Cambridge,

    MA: Harvard University Press.

McAdams, D. P. (1989). The development of a narrative

    identity. In D. M. Buss, & N. Cantor (Eds.),

    Personality psychology: Recent trends and emerging

    directions (pp. 124-132). New York: Springer-Verlag.

Spence, D. P. (1984). *Narrative truth and historical truth*.

    New York: Norton.

Swanson, H. Lee (1999). What develops in working memory? A

    life span perspective. *Developmental Psychology, 35*,

    986-1000. Retrieved March 12, 2000 from the World Wide

    Web: http://www.apa.org/journals/dev/dev354986.html

Webster, J. D., & Young, R. A. (1988). Process variables of

    the life review: Counselling implications.

    International Journal of Aging and Human Development,

    26, 315-323.

DOUBLE SPACE

1 INCH MARGINS

THE NOTE STYLE OF DOCUMENTATION

Although parenthetical text-referencing and author-date systems of documentation are widely used, in some courses (e.g., History and Political Science) you may be required to use numbered footnotes or endnotes to acknowledge sources. Many books and articles employ this traditional method, so you should familiarize yourself with its basic conventions, in any case.

Ask your instructor whether you should use footnotes or endnotes. In general, the more notes you have, the more practical it is to gather them together as endnotes at the end of the text.

Placement of Notes and Note Numbers

In the note system, quotations, paraphrases, and other uses of source material are numbered consecutively from [1] throughout the text with arabic superscripts (numbers that go a half space above the line). They are then acknowledged in correspondingly numbered notes that appear either at the foot of the text pages, or on a separate page (or pages) under the heading `Notes` immediately following the end of the text. Good word-processing programs will help you create footnotes and endnotes, handling the placing of superscript numbers and the spacing of lines.

The guidelines below mainly follow Chicago note style.

1. Place a superscript number in your text immediately following any phrase, clause, or sentence that contains quoted, paraphrased, or summarized material.
2. Place the number outside any final punctuation (except a dash).
3. Leave a letter space after the number but not in front of it.
4. Do not punctuate the number in any way.
5. Match this text number to a full-sized footnote number at the foot of the page, or to a full-sized endnote number on a separate page at the end of the text.
6. Place a period after the number, followed by one letter space, and then write the note.

See the following sample page (page 109) showing the placement of numbers in the text and the corresponding footnotes.

Content of First Notes

For the first reference to a book, give full details. Include in the note the author's full name as given on the title page; the title, including the subtitle (if any), underlined (but check to see if your instructor prefers italics); the name of an editor or translator (if any); the volume and edition numbers (if any); the city of publication; the publisher's name in full (omitting "Co.," "Ltd.," etc.); the date of publication; and the page number of the reference. Provide corresponding information for other works—see the sample entries that follow.

Note Layout

1. Begin footnotes two line spaces below the text.
2. Indent the first line of a note five spaces from the left margin; begin subsequent lines at the margin.
3. Double space footnotes and endnotes. Double space between entries. Some instructors may, however, prefer the notes to be single spaced with a double space between them. If in doubt, ask.
4. Leave one letter space between the period after the number and the beginning of the note.
5. First and last names of authors appear in the normal order.
6. Place a comma between the author's name and the title of the work, and between the publisher's name and the date of publication. Put parentheses around the city of publication, the publisher, and the year of publication. Place a colon followed by one letter space between the city of publication and the publisher's name. Be sure to put a period at the end of the entry. Leave only one letter space between major parts of the note.
7. Do *not* use the abbreviations "p.", "pp." or "pg." before the page number(s).

Subsequent Notes

The first time you acknowledge a source, provide full details, as indicated above. For *all* subsequent references to the same source, use an abbreviated form of the note, typically the author's last name followed by a comma and the page number(s). Note 13 on the sample text page is a second reference to the same page in *The Coming of War* by May, and cited immediately above in note 12.

Although separated by other references, note 15 on the sample page also refers the reader to note 12.

If you had referred to two works by May, then you would distinguish between them in a subsequent note by including an abbreviated form of the title:

```
15. May, Coming, 48.
```

Note Terms and Abbreviations

The traditional note style employed Latin abbreviations to indicate subsequent references in footnotes. Most authorities recommend against their continued use preferring the simple repetition of an author's last name, plus a page number (although the Chicago *Manual* sanctions the use of "ibid"). But since they appear in already published works, you should understand their meaning:

ibid. (*ibidem*)
means "in the same place." It is used when references to a particular source follow one another immediately, with no other reference intervening.

loc. cit. (*loco citato*)
means "in the place (or passage) cited," i.e., in the same passage referred to in a nearby note. It is preceded by an author's name, in the note or in the text, but is not followed by a page number since the passage has already been identified in the previous note.

op. cit. (*opere citato*)
means "in the work cited." It is used when referring to a passage on a different page of a work noted nearby. Again it is preceded by an author's name in note or text, but this time a new page number appears.

A Latin abbreviation still in use in both the parenthetical and note systems of referencing is "et al." (*et alii*), meaning "and others"; it is used to refer to a work with more than three authors.

Bibliographic Citations

In the note style of documentation, the list of bibliographic citations is called a "Bibliography." To prepare it, centre the word `Bibliography` half an inch below the page number and list entries alphabetically by the last name of the first author mentioned in the work's publishing information.

Sample Notes and Citations

Punctuate notes and bibliographic citations carefully using the following examples (note followed by citation) as models. In general, the main items in a note are separated by commas, while the main items in a bibliographic citation are separated by periods. In a note, the city of publication and the publisher are in parentheses; in a bibliographic citation they are not. Double space notes and citations (and also between entries) unless your instructor prefers them to be single spaced. If in doubt, ask.

○ BOOK WITH ONE AUTHOR

```
    1. W. J. Reader, Life in Victorian England (London:
Batsford, 1964) 42.
```

```
Reader, W. J. Life in Victorian England. London: Batsford,
    1964.
```

○ BOOK WITH MORE THAN THREE AUTHORS

```
    2. Yuko Shibata et al., The Forgotten History of
the Japanese Canadians, vol. 1 (Vancouver: New Sun Press,
1977) 10.
```

```
Shibata, Yuko, et al. The Forgotten History of the
    Japanese Canadians. Vol. 1. Vancouver: New Sun Press,
    1977.
```

BOOK WITH EDITOR

3. Veronica Strong-Boag, ed., A Woman with a Purpose: The Diaries of Elizabeth Smith, 1872-1884 (Toronto: University of Toronto Press, 1980) 102.

Strong-Boag, Veronica, ed. A Woman with a Purpose: The Diaries of Elizabeth Smith, 1872-1884. Toronto: University of Toronto Press, 1980.

BOOK ONLINE

4. Plato, The Republic, trans. Benjamin Jowett, http://classics.mit.edu/Plato/republic.5.iv.html (April 3, 2000).

Plato. The Republic. Translated by Benjamin Jowett. http://classics.mit.edu/Plato/republic.5.iv.html (April 3, 2000).

ESSAY IN AN ANTHOLOGY

5. L. J. Evenden and I. D. Anderson, "The Presence of a Past Community: Tashme, British Columbia," Peoples of the Living Land, ed. Julian V. Minghi (Vancouver: Tantalus Press, 1972) 63.

Evenden, L. J., and I. D. Anderson. "The Presence of a Past Community: Tashme, British Columbia." Peoples of the Living Land, edited by Julian V. Minghi. Vancouver: Tantalus Press, 1972. 58-72.

ARTICLE IN A JOURNAL WITH A VOLUME NUMBER

6. Chad Gaffield, "Children, Schooling, and Family Reproduction in Nineteenth Century Ontario," Canadian Historical Review 72 (June 1991): 162.

```
Gaffield, Chad. "Children, Schooling, and Family
       Reproduction in Nineteenth Century Ontario." Canadian
       Historical Review 72 (June 1991): 157-91.
```

Note: in this journal, pagination is continuous within each volume, so the issue number is omitted. If each issue of a journal is paginated separately, put a period after the volume number and add the issue number, e.g., 72.2. Add the date of issue in parentheses after the volume number.

○ ARTICLE IN A JOURNAL ONLINE

```
       7. James Henretta, "Margaret Brent: A Woman of
Property," Early America Review 2.3 (1998),
http://earlyamerica.com/review/1998/brent.html(March 15,
2000).

Henretta, James. "Margaret Brent: A Woman of Property."
       Early America Review 2.3 (1998).
       http://earlyamerica.com/review/1998/brent.html (March
       15, 2000).
```

Note: here the volume number "2" has been converted from Roman numeral "II" in the original source.

○ ARTICLE IN A WEEKLY OR MONTHLY MAGAZINE

```
       8. Roger Rosenblatt, "What Really Mattered? Not Just
Great Events But Underlying Causes," Time October 5, 1983:
22.

Rosenblatt, Roger. "What Really Mattered? Not Just Great
       Events But Underlying Causes." Time October 5, 1983:
       22-25.

       9. Kishu Singh and Dilip Bobb, "Perishtroika, Mon
Amour," New Internationalist September 1990: 20.

Singh, Kishu, and Dilip Bobb. "Perishtroika, Mon Amour."
       New Internationalist September 1990: 19-20.
```

Note: indicate the issue by date alone; omit volume and issue numbers.

○ **ARTICLE IN A NEWSPAPER** (no author's name given)

> 10. "West Begins Recognizing Baltic States," <u>Globe and Mail</u> August 26, 1991: A1.

> "West Begins Recognizing Baltic States." <u>Globe and Mail</u> August 26, 1991: A1.

Note: begin with the author's name, if it is given.

○ **ARTICLE IN AN ENCYCLOPEDIA** (author's name given)

> 11. Donald MacGillivray Nicol, "Byzantine Empire," <u>The New Encyclopaedia Britannica: Macropaedia</u>, 15th ed., 2002.

> Nicol, Donald MacGillivray. "Byzantine Empire." <u>The New Encyclopaedia Britannica: Macropaedia</u>. 15th ed. 2002.

Note: this article is signed at the end with initials only. To find the name of the author, look up "D.M.N." in the volume entitled *Propaedia: Guide to the Britannica*. To find the article, look up the alphabetized title. Because articles are alphabetized throughout the work, volume and page numbers are omitted.

○ **PARLIAMENTARY DEBATE**

> 12. Canada, House of Commons, <u>Debates, Official Report</u>, 32nd Parliament, 1st session, vol. 5 (Ottawa: Queen's Printer, 1980): 5537.

> Canada. Parliament. House of Commons. <u>Debates, Official Report</u>. 32nd Parliament. 1st session. Vol. 5. Ottawa: Queen's Printer, 1980.

Sample Text Page (Note Style)

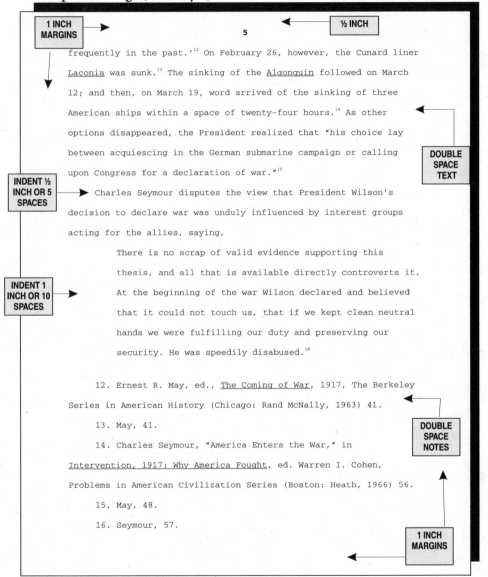

1 INCH MARGINS

½ INCH

5

frequently in the past."[12] On February 26, however, the Cunard liner Laconia was sunk.[13] The sinking of the Algonquin followed on March 12; and then, on March 19, word arrived of the sinking of three American ships within a space of twenty-four hours.[14] As other options disappeared, the President realized that "his choice lay between acquiescing in the German submarine campaign or calling upon Congress for a declaration of war."[15]

DOUBLE SPACE TEXT

INDENT ½ INCH OR 5 SPACES

Charles Seymour disputes the view that President Wilson's decision to declare war was unduly influenced by interest groups acting for the allies, saying,

INDENT 1 INCH OR 10 SPACES

> There is no scrap of valid evidence supporting this thesis, and all that is available directly controverts it. At the beginning of the war Wilson declared and believed that it could not touch us, that if we kept clean neutral hands we were fulfilling our duty and preserving our security. He was speedily disabused.[16]

12. Ernest R. May, ed., The Coming of War, 1917, The Berkeley Series in American History (Chicago: Rand McNally, 1963) 41.

13. May, 41.

DOUBLE SPACE NOTES

14. Charles Seymour, "America Enters the War," in Intervention, 1917: Why America Fought, ed. Warren I. Cohen, Problems in American Civilization Series (Boston: Heath, 1966) 56.

15. May, 48.

16. Seymour, 57.

1 INCH MARGINS

INDEX